Who Is an Evangelical?

Who Is an Evangelical?

The History of a Movement in Crisis

THOMAS S. KIDD

Yale UNIVERSITY PRESS

New Haven and London

Published with assistance from the Mary Cady Tew Memorial Fund.

Yale University Press books may be purchased in quantity for educational, business, or promotional use. For information, please e-mail sales.press@yale.edu (U.S. office) or sales@yaleup.co.uk (U.K. office).

Set in Minion type by IDS Infotech Ltd., Chandigarh, India.
Printed in the United States of America.

Library of Congress Control Number: 2019933835

ISBN 978-0-300-24141-9 (hardcover : alk. paper)

A catalogue record for this book is available from the British Library.

This paper meets the requirements of ANSI/NISO Z39.48-1992 (Permanence of Paper).

10 9 8 7 6 5 4 3 2 1

Blessed be the God and Father of our Lord Jesus Christ! According to his great mercy, he has caused us to be born again to a living hope through the resurrection of Jesus Christ from the dead.

1 PETER 1:3 (English Standard Version)

Contents

Introduction

Who Is an Evangelical? is an introduction to what is arguably America's most controversial religious movement. The word *evangelical* itself is a source of confusion: scholars, journalists, and the public can't seem to decide what it means. (I will explain what I mean by it momentarily.) Nonevangelical people who follow the news may have a variety of impressions about what the term suggests. But one certain association people make with the word is *Republican*. The term *evangelical* has become fundamentally political in popular parlance. Another likely association is *white*. Many may recall that around 81 percent of self-described white evangelicals voted for Donald Trump. Polls and stories about evangelical political behavior almost always assume the evangelicals in question are white. Some polls don't account for any other kind of evangelical.[1]

This book seeks to show how historically peculiar a partisan and ethnic definition of evangelicals is. It also explains what went wrong with the public understanding of evangelicals, and how a group of what I will call "Republican insider evangelicals" abetted the politicization of the movement.

Today's crisis of evangelicalism is rooted in the movement's history. But the crisis became increasingly conspicuous after World War II, grew more acute during the Moral Majority era of the 1980s, and then broke wide open with the 2016 election of Donald Trump. The evangelical crisis has several overlapping facets, including (1) confusion about the term, (2) an impression that "evangelical" may just mean white Republicans who consider themselves religious, (3) a sense that political power may be the essential evangelical agenda, and (4) the inability of evangelicals of different ethnicities, especially whites and blacks, to agree on basic political questions.

I am not a disinterested observer of this crisis. In addition to being an academic historian, I am a white evangelical myself. I experienced spiritual conversion in my teens, and since then I have been involved in a variety of evangelical parachurch ministries and churches. For the past two decades, I have been active in a conservative Baptist church in Waco, Texas, where I teach an adult Sunday school class. I am one of the few people in my church who would regularly use the word *evangelical*, though. Others, when pressed, might describe themselves as "Baptist" or "Bible-believing" or "born again."

Evangelical is a scholarly and journalistic term that doesn't resonate with many laypeople (especially nonwhites), including those who do appear to be evangelicals according to standard definitions. Trying to pin down evangelicals can be maddening: some Christians who seem to be evangelicals do not describe themselves as such. Others (especially whites) who don't necessarily hold evangelical beliefs or regularly attend church nonetheless tell pollsters that they *are* evangelicals. As we proceed, I will examine why this might be.

I also blog at the evangelical website The Gospel Coalition and have written for outlets such as *Vox* and the *Washington Post* about evangelicals and politics. In publicly exploring the evangelical crisis, I have deplored the turn that many white evangelicals took in the 2016 election. I am a #NeverTrump evangelical. Though I had never been a straight-ticket voter, I usually voted Republican in elections prior to 2016. But in that year, I voted for neither the Republican nor the Democratic presidential nominee. I believe that something has gone terribly wrong in much of white evangelical culture, though I remain as committed as ever to historic evangelical beliefs and practices. I will keep going to my evangelical church, but at the moment I am politically homeless.

This book is an attempt to introduce readers to evangelicals' experiences, practices, and beliefs, and to examine the reasons for our crisis today. I hope that scholars will find the book valuable, but it is mainly written for other people—journalists, pastors, people who work in politics, and more—who are interested in what makes evangelicals tick. *Who Is an Evangelical?* is for people who might ask, "What has happened to evangelicals?" They were supposedly a religious movement, but now they seem to show up only on Election Day to vote Republican, regardless of who that Republican is. My hope is that this book will show that there is far more to the evangelical story. The narrative of white evangelicals' corrupt quest for Republican power is not false. But it is incomplete.

This is an *introduction* to evangelicals. A full account of the evangelical movement would have to be much longer, and would detail the phenomenal global expansion of evangelical and Pentecostal faith over the past century.[2] In contrast, my account is focused on North America and is deliberately limited in scope. Specialists may be disappointed that I don't give attention to certain evangelical or Pentecostal leaders. My intention is not to slight any aspect of evangelical history, but simply to provide a primer that is as useful as possible.

Evangelicalism was multiethnic from the beginning. This is one of the reasons that the refrain of "evangelical" support for Donald Trump is problematic. Hispanic, African American, and other evangelical people of color are just as evangelical as white evangelicals are. Sometimes nonwhite evangelicals seem more consistent in their beliefs and actions than white evangelicals. My intention is that whites do not appear in this book, implicitly or explicitly, as the "normal" evangelicals. Especially in a global perspective, as evangelicals and Pentecostals have forged centers of evangelical strength in Latin America, Africa, and Asia, white English speakers are just one evangelical cohort among many. But they're a cohort with disproportionate power and resources.

What does it mean to be evangelical? The simple answer is that evangelical Christianity is the *religion of the born again.* I will explain more about the term *born again* in the chapters to come. For now, I'll say that being born again is the conversion experience that defines what it means to be an evangelical. The great English Methodist John Wesley wrote that conversion is "a thorough change of heart and life from sin to holiness; a turning."[3] This turning, to evangelicals, is enabled by God's power.

Here's a more detailed definition: *Evangelicals are born-again Protestants who cherish the Bible as the Word of God and who emphasize a personal relationship with Jesus Christ through the Holy Spirit.* This definition hinges upon three aspects of what it means to be an evangelical: being born again, the primacy of the Bible, and the divine presence of God the Son and God the Holy Spirit. As we shall see, evangelicals of the mid-1700s saw themselves as different from other Protestants because of their born-again experience and the way that they "walked" with the Holy Spirit, the third person of the divine

Trinity. More recent evangelicals (especially non-Pentecostals) have tended to speak about their "personal relationship with Jesus," terminology that became common among Protestants in the 1880s.[4] In both cases, God's discernible presence is key. As anthropologist Tanya Luhrmann puts it, the "feature that most deeply characterizes [evangelicals] is that the God they seek is more personally intimate, and more intimately experienced, than the God most Americans grew up with." This intimacy with God has marked evangelicals since the 1700s.[5]

Evangelicals' emphasis on the Bible did not originally set them apart from most other Protestants, as *sola scriptura* (the Bible as faith's final authority) was one of the defining beliefs of the Protestant Reformers of the 1500s. But by the early twentieth century, evangelicals came to see themselves as distinguished from theological "modernists" who questioned the reliability of the Bible. Because of the fundamentalist-modernist controversy of the 1920s, the doctrine of the Bible's "inerrancy" (its entire veracity in all details) became an evangelical hallmark.

Defining evangelicalism in this tripartite way—conversion, Bible, and divine presence—means that I also include Pentecostals as evangelicals. This is a disputed issue. Pentecostals and evangelicals have substantial theological disagreements, and one could justify separating them historically. Evangelicals and Pentecostals both affirm the authority of the Bible, the need to be born again, and the believer's vital connection to Jesus through the Holy Spirit. But they part ways on what to expect from the Spirit. In particular, Pentecostals believe that the experience of the "baptism" of the Holy Spirit is separate from being born again. When a Pentecostal believer receives the baptism of the Spirit, it is typically marked by glossolalia, or speaking in tongues. Non-Pentecostal evangelicals believe that the baptism of the Spirit occurs at conversion, not after it.

Moreover, starting in the 1960s there was a powerful "charismatic" renewal movement that swept across Catholic, mainline Protestant, and evangelical churches. That movement blurred lines between Pentecostals and non-Pentecostals, even though many of the new charismatics didn't put as much emphasis as Pentecostals on speaking in tongues.

Thus, many evangelicals engage in exuberant worship, expect miraculous healings, and exhibit other Pentecostal tendencies. But they don't usually affirm a separate baptism of the Spirit marked by tongues. All Pentecostals are charismatics, but only some evangelicals are charismatics. "Cessationist" evangelicals say that dramatic gifts of the Spirit, such as tongues, ceased to operate after the apostolic period of early Christianity.

Evangelicals disagree with each other about a host of theological, cultural, and political issues, so disagreements don't necessarily require that we exclude anyone from the fold, assuming that they share basic evangelical characteristics. There was no clear evangelical/Pentecostal division prior to the 1906 Azusa Street Revival in Los Angeles, which marked the beginning of the modern Pentecostal movement. Many evangelicals in the 1700s and 1800s made much of the Spirit, sometimes in ways that sounded Pentecostal. Over the past hundred years, many of the Hispanics and African Americans who are most visibly evangelical have technically been Pentecostals, as are many whites in denominations such as the Assemblies of God. Even cessationists and Pentecostals share a great deal in common in the evangelical tradition. If evangelicals and Pentecostals today don't always act like brothers and sisters, they nevertheless remain cousins.

One important religious group I *do not* focus on here is the "prosperity gospel" movement, a popular and controversial outgrowth of Pentecostalism. Prosperity gospel teachers assert that the proper exercise of faith will inexorably lead to health, wealth, and "victorious living." Most outside observers lump in pastors such as Joel Osteen, Joyce Meyer, T. D. Jakes, and Paula White (who is the most visible of President Trump's religious advisors) with evangelicals. But there are good reasons not to concentrate on them in this book. Although many prosperity gospel churches emerged from the Pentecostal tradition, their theology has so dramatically departed from historic Pentecostalism that many Pentecostal leaders distance themselves from the prosperity gospel preachers. In some cases, what historian Kate Bowler has called "hard prosperity" teaching becomes unmoored not only from evangelical beliefs but from traditional Christian themes such as atonement for sin, the need for divine forgiveness, the reality of suffering, and the final importance of eternity rather than material success in this life. And while "cessationist" evangelicals have serious misgivings about some Pentecostal practices (especially speaking in tongues), a much larger segment of evangelicals see the prosperity gospel as un-Christian charlatanism. You can find versions of "soft prosperity" teachings in many evangelical and Pentecostal churches, but I have largely chosen to exclude hard-edged prosperity gospel churches from the story I am telling here.[6]

1

The Rise of Evangelicals

Where did evangelicals come from? Many evangelicals would probably say, "We came from Jesus" and leave it at that. Evangelicals don't have the market cornered on this "primitivist" impulse to connect their movement to Christianity's origins. Many groups of Christians envision themselves as the purest inheritors of the movement Jesus founded. One online religious retailer, for example, offers a T-shirt with the slogan "Catholic Church—Founded 33 A.D." emblazoned on it.

Still, any evangelical Christian would say that his or her faith is based on the teachings of Christ and his disciples, as recorded in the Bible. The rub comes when you have to interpret what the Bible says about disputed points of that faith. For example, what does the Bible teach about church leadership? What is the biblical mode of baptism? Just those two questions have precipitated centuries of churchly conflict, and sometimes even bloodshed.

The term *evangelical* is based on the Greek word *euangelion*, meaning "good news" or "gospel." We speak of the first four books of the New Testament as "gospels," and the Gospel of Mark 1:15 records Jesus as saying, "The time is fulfilled, and the kingdom of God is at hand: repent ye, and believe the *gospel*" (unless otherwise noted, all Scripture quotations are from the King James Version). The Greek *euangelion* was a noun in the New Testament. In Germany during the Protestant Reformation of the 1500s, the word *evangelisch* came to denote "Protestant." Until the early 1800s, English-speaking people typically used "evangelical" as an adjective, as in "evangelical faith."

In 1807, the English poet Robert Southey became one of the first writers ever to use the noun "evangelicals" in print. When he penned the word, Southey was musing on the problem of "enthusiasm." At that time, enthusiasm meant religious frenzy, a characteristic Southey applied to the early Methodist movement, initially led by the great evangelical preachers John Wesley and George Whitefield in the mid-1700s. Wesley was the eighteenth century's greatest religious organizer, but Whitefield was the era's most famous preacher. Indeed, by the early 1740s Whitefield was arguably the most famous person in Britain and America (or at least the most famous person not named King George). Whitefield found his key patron in the person of Selina Hastings, the Countess of Huntingdon. Whitefield's "preachers were usually called by [Huntingdon's] name," Southey wrote, the "Countess's Connexion." But the preachers who followed in Whitefield's massive wake had largely abandoned that association, Southey noted, choosing instead "the better title of Evangelicals."[1]

By the time Southey was writing in 1807, "evangelicals" in Britain and America had represented a distinctive, transdenominational movement for seventy years. In the early 1800s, the word began to shift from adjective to noun. "Evangelicals," in short, were Christians who believed in the message preached by George Whitefield and his successors. Whitefield's message

was that all people—regardless of church membership, ethnicity, or social standing—needed the "new birth" of salvation
through Jesus Christ. The Holy Spirit would change the hearts
of true believers, empowering them to live God-honoring lives.
The Holy Spirit, Whitefield taught, was working all over the
world, precipitating revivals in which unconverted people experienced the new birth. Already converted people also had
their faith renewed in revivals.

At their founding moment, then, evangelicals believed in
the new birth of salvation and the presence of the Holy Spirit,
and they worked and prayed for revival. In accord with the
norms of the era, white people tended to lead the evangelical
movement. Many of those white people had manifest failings,
including owning slaves. But white evangelical leaders also gave
unprecedented latitude to the voices of African Americans and
Native Americans. Some evangelicals, such as the former slave
trader John Newton (the author of the hymn "Amazing Grace"),
did become involved in political causes such as abolitionism.
The line separating "spiritual" and "political" was always blurry
and contested for evangelicals. But there was no doubt that
evangelicalism was, at root, a spiritual movement. The extent
and focus of evangelical political engagement have changed
over time, and different evangelical ethnic groups have prioritized different issues. But historically, the evangelical movement
was defined by the message of conversion and eternal salvation,
not partisan politics.

For evangelicals, the Bible's good news is that Jesus Christ, the
Son of God, has come to save sinners. Many nonevangelical
Christians would likewise affirm this claim as a central message
of the Bible. But some Christians have put more emphasis than
evangelicals on Jesus as a moral exemplar (Jesus came to show

us how to live) or the institutional church (Jesus came to establish his church). Conversely, some Christians would not put as much emphasis on humankind's sinfulness or on the threat of God's judgment against sinners.

God's wrath is the reason evangelicals and other traditional Christians say that people need to be "saved." Saved from what? Saved from hell. God's holiness is so perfect, evangelicals contend, that he cannot overlook sin. His perfect justice demands eternal punishment for rebellious sinners. As a good judge and perfect being, God must hold lawbreakers accountable. But unlike a human judge, God's judgments are eternal. The Bible speaks routinely of the need for salvation. Indeed, Christ's own teachings on salvation seemed so stringent that his disciples almost despaired, asking him in Matthew 19:25, "Who then can be saved?"

Jesus replied that "with men this is impossible; but with God all things are possible." Men and women cannot save themselves, evangelicals say. Only God can do that. How does God save people? The same God who is wrathful and perfect in justice is also merciful. Jesus, as the Son of God and second person of the divine Trinity, came to offer sinners mercy and forgiveness. But God could not unilaterally forgive people because that would undermine his justice. (He would be like a judge who, in an impetuous fit of mercy, decides to "let off" an accused felon, even though he or she is clearly guilty.) Instead, God the Father sent Jesus the Son to live a perfect life on earth. When Jesus died a criminal's death on the cross, he took on himself the penalty of sin that sinners deserved. Providing "atonement" for sin, Jesus's death freed God the Father morally to forgive those who believe. As Timothy Keller of New York's Redeemer Presbyterian Church has explained, "The essence of the atonement is always Jesus acting as our substitute.

. . . Jesus does for us what we cannot do for ourselves."[2] After his death, Jesus was buried but rose from the dead to show that he was victorious over death and sin. In these beliefs, evangelicals draw from deep wells within the broader Christian tradition.

A more distinctive belief of evangelicals is that the key moment in an individual's salvation is the "new birth." This term does not appear in the King James Bible, but it was common in English parlance before the Great Awakening in the 1740s. The new birth refers to being born again, an experience that Jesus described in the Gospel of John. John 3:16 is one of the best-known verses in the Bible: "For God so loved the world, that he gave his only begotten Son, that whosoever believeth in him should not perish, but have everlasting life." The verse is a common choice of evangelicals, who put it on everything from T-shirts to banners at football games.

John 3:3 is of even more precise importance to evangelicals, though. That passage describes a Pharisee named Nicodemus who had come to Jesus by night, confessing that he knew Jesus's teachings were from God. Jesus told Nicodemus that appreciating his teaching was not enough. Jesus "said unto him, 'Verily, verily, I say unto thee, except a man be born again, he cannot see the kingdom of God.'" Nicodemus was perplexed by this teaching. "How can a man be born when he is old?" the Pharisee asked. Jesus explained that "except a man be born of water and of the Spirit, he cannot enter into the kingdom of God. That which is born of the flesh is flesh; and that which is born of the Spirit is spirit. Marvel not that I said unto thee, Ye must be born again." (John 3:4–7)

The Bible does not provide a great deal more information about the born-again experience, aside from a reference to it in I Peter 1:23. But theologians have routinely connected being born again to *regeneration*, or the Holy Spirit's transformation of a believer's inner nature, referenced in Titus 3:5. Nicodemus was confused about how a person could be born again; readers might likewise find the concept puzzling. Jesus noted that it doesn't happen to everyone. All people have the first, physical birth. But only true Christian believers have the second, spiritual birth. This is what the popular Christmas hymn "Hark the Herald Angels Sing," written by Charles Wesley and George Whitefield, refers to when it says that Jesus was "Born to raise the sons of earth; / Born to give them second birth."

Before the Protestant Reformation of the 1500s, Christians often believed that baptism marked the moment of regeneration. Before the early 1600s, virtually all Christians practiced infant baptism instead of "believer's baptism." Baptizing people *after* their profession of faith started to become a known practice among Protestants during the 1600s, becoming far more common with the growth of Baptist, Pentecostal, and nondenominational churches in the 1900s. Even after he revolted against the Catholic Church, the great German Reformer Martin Luther still linked the sacrament of baptism to regeneration. But Luther also believed that Christians needed to consciously accept God's grace for themselves when old enough to understand the gospel.[3]

Certain Reformers in the 1500s separated infant baptism from the new birth, however. Huldrych Zwingli, a leading Swiss Reformer, insisted that baptism was symbolic and that it could not bring about regeneration or the new birth. "Baptism cannot confirm faith in infants," Zwingli wrote, "because infants are not able to believe." Saving faith was the gift of God alone, not the result of a sacrament or parents' obedience. Zwingli would not go as far as some of the radical Anabaptists, who condemned infant baptism altogether. The Anabaptists rebaptized their members because they said that their baptism as infants was invalid. Many Reformers regarded the Anabaptists (usually called "Baptists" by English speakers) as reckless incendiaries who sought to tear apart Europe's Christian societies.[4]

During the 1500s and 1600s the Reformed ancestors of evangelicals struggled to understand the timing and means of the new birth. In England, the Puritans were the most intense partisans of the Reformation. Though they continued to affirm infant baptism, many Puritans disconnected baptism from the new birth. Thomas Hooker, the founder of the Connecticut colony, briefly spent time as a refugee pastor in the Netherlands before going to the New World. He rejected the Book of Common Prayer's baptismal rites when he went to the Netherlands because the Church of England's prayer book affirmed baptismal regeneration. Indeed, Hooker used no prepared script when he baptized infants; he said that he simply spoke as the Spirit led. He would never baptize infants until he could confirm that the child's parents were faithful believers. Hooker and many Puritans made a stark distinction between "outward" conformity to the rituals of the church and the "inward" transformation required for salvation.[5]

Today, American evangelicals tend to be much more "baptistic" than they were in the 1740s. In other words, it is more common now for evangelicals to practice believer's baptism than infant baptism, even if they are not technically part of a Baptist church. In the 1600s, Anabaptists and English Baptists began to clear up the connection between baptism and regeneration. (In this discussion remember that I am a Baptist, so I am biased.) Baptists argued that no one should receive baptism unless there were hopeful signs that they had undergone the new birth. These signs included profession of new faith in Christ, repentance of sins, and love for God, the Bible, and church members. Most in the Reformed community would not go this far on baptism in the 1600s and 1700s. But for the emerging evangelical movement, the separation of the new birth from infant baptism was essential. For evangelicals (even those like George Whitefield and Jonathan Edwards, who affirmed infant baptism), the new birth could happen only to people who understood their need for salvation.

A number of theological and cultural factors converged in the late 1600s and early 1700s to forge the new evangelical movement. One was a focus on individuals. As the "modern" age began to dawn, the people of Europe, Britain, and the American colonies started to appraise people as individuals rather than just as parts of families and communities. The trend toward individualism was a complex change, but most scholars see this as a key development separating the medieval from the modern era. As philosopher Charles Taylor has written, humankind's older "self-understanding was deeply embedded in society. Our essential identity was as father, son, etc., and member of this tribe. Only later did we come to conceive ourselves as free individuals first."[6]

Christianity contained the seeds of individualism from the beginning. Even the lowliest people in society could become children of God through Christ, giving all Christians a basic claim on individual dignity. Historians have also argued that the Renaissance, the Reformation, and the Enlightenment boosted Western culture's emerging focus on discrete persons.

Evangelical Christianity's chief tributaries also highlighted the religious experience of the individual. The most important of these were Pietist movements flowing from the Reformation. European Pietists emphasized not just correct doctrine or church government but heartfelt love for God, and

God's discernible presence. Johann Arndt, a Lutheran theologian in the early 1600s, was one of the founders of Pietism. Arndt bridged the Reformation to Pietism and evangelicalism, as he had been a student of the great German Reformer Philip Melanchthon. He saw the new birth as the beginning of true faith. "The new birth," Arndt wrote in his classic book, *True Christianity* (1605–10), "is a work of God the Holy Spirit through which our heart, sense and mind, reason, will and emotions are changed and renewed, in and according to Christ Jesus, into a new creature." Arndt's ideas spread across Europe, from England to Russia, during the seventeenth and eighteenth centuries. The English Great Awakening leaders John Wesley and George Whitefield both discovered Arndt's *True Christianity* in the year 1736. By that time the book had gone through 125 printings and had been translated from German at least nine times. Aside from the Bible, no other book has circulated more widely in the history of Protestant Christianity. Its focus on the new birth would frame evangelical faith.[7]

The Reformation had renewed the doctrine of salvation by grace alone. But the Reformed churches of the Continent, England, and Scotland were also riven by terrible disagreements over the Lord's Supper, baptism, and the proper mode of church government. Was Christ literally present in the bread and wine of the Lord's Supper? Should churches continue to appoint leaders, whether bishops or presbyters, to give oversight to individual congregations? Protestants (Lutherans versus Calvinists, Congregationalists versus High Church Anglicans, and so on) fought with each other over such matters, sometimes as stridently as they fought with their Catholic rivals.

Pietists did not ignore such intra-Protestant debates, but they did herald a new pan-Protestant unity based on the "religion of the heart." Pietists prized an individual man's or woman's religious experience more than churchly debates about sacraments and governance. Europe's overseas colonies, especially in North America, proved ideal locations for piety focused on individual experience more than church structure and liturgy. In general, the American colonies had weaker "established" (or government-supported) churches than did European countries. There was more room in America for personal religious expression. America is not where evangelical faith began. It began among European Pietists. But America is where evangelical faith would first reach full bloom.[8]

The new evangelical movement heavily emphasized the believer's experience of the new birth. The new birth also led into a relationship with God mediated by the Holy Spirit, or "Holy Ghost" in King James Bible terminology. Jesus had promised that the Father would send the Holy Spirit once Jesus had ascended into heaven. "The Comforter, which is the Holy Ghost, whom the Father will send in my name, he shall teach you all things," Jesus said in the Gospel of John. Throughout Christian history, some have emphasized the "felt presence" of the Holy Spirit as a source of comfort, revelation, and power. Medieval Catholic mystics such as the English anchoress Julian of Norwich regularly attributed their ecstatic transports to the Holy Spirit. In the late 1300s, Julian credited her intimacy with Christ to a "special revelation from our Lord" or "a great abundance of grace given inwardly by the Holy Spirit."[9]

Naturalist philosophers in the seventeenth and eighteenth centuries pushed God's existence to the margins of lived experience. Pietists and the new evangelicals reacted to naturalism by putting a premium on God's presence in everyday life. As the great English hymn writer Isaac Watts put it in a prayerful song,

Come, Holy Spirit, Heav'nly Dove,
With all thy quick'ning Pow'rs
Kindle a Flame of sacred Love
In these cold Hearts of ours.

Skeptical observers then and now see this talk about experienc-
ing God as just that—talk. More technically, they see this
God-talk as a "folk hermeneutics" that makes "the Bible true
and Jesus real." Hostile analysts would contend that an evangelical's friendship with Jesus and walk in the Spirit are delu-
sional at best. I won't belabor my account with constant
references to skeptics' doubts, but I do want to acknowledge
them here.[10]

Pietists certainly saw some adherents run to extremes in
their belief that the Spirit would speak to their souls. The
Spirit's role was one of the core issues in the "Antinomian Controversy" in 1630s Massachusetts. The gifted lay teacher Anne
Hutchinson criticized most of Boston's pastors for (she said)
implicitly teaching that salvation was the result not of grace but
of obedience to God. When on trial before Massachusetts
founder John Winthrop, Hutchinson confessed that she had
gotten her insights from the Holy Spirit. This statement was
enough to earn her banishment to Rhode Island, where Puritan
authorities sent many dissenters.[11]

Hutchinson's intense dependence on the Spirit was
frowned upon by many Puritans. But by the 1730s, growing
numbers of Protestants saw vital communion with the Spirit as
a mark of true Christianity. Some pastors in Europe and
America started to believe that what their societies needed was
an "outpouring" of the Spirit to generate revival. The new evangelicals emphasized the work of the Spirit in discrete believers,
but also on a corporate basis. The individual sinner needed the

Spirit to regenerate his or her soul, giving the sinner a new God-ward inclination. Believers could also expect the Spirit to guide them in discernible ways as they sought to live out their faith.

But many church leaders in the early 1700s also hoped that the Spirit might bring revival, leading to large numbers of conversions (as well as rededications of those who had fallen away from God) at one time. Revival preachers turned to passages such as Isaiah 44:3, where God promised, "I will pour my spirit upon thy seed, and my blessing upon thine offspring." They also referred to Joel 2:28–29: "I will pour out my spirit upon all flesh; and your sons and your daughters shall prophesy, your old men shall dream dreams, your young men shall see visions: And also upon the servants and upon the handmaids in those days will I pour out my spirit." Isaiah 44:3 became one of the most commonly cited Bible verses during the Great Awakening of the mid-eighteenth century. Joel 2 also appeared routinely. But verses like Joel 2:28–29 made some traditionalist pastors nervous because of the image of the Spirit being poured out on daughters, servants, and handmaids. Moderate evangelical leaders eagerly welcomed the Spirit's converting work. But an outpouring of the Holy Ghost on women and lowly people reminded them too much of antinomian (lawless) episodes like that of Anne Hutchinson.[12]

When evangelical Christianity was in its founding years, conversion and God's discernible presence were evangelicals' signature experiences. Historian David Bebbington, who has crafted the most commonly cited definition of "evangelical," argues that conversionism, biblicism, activism, and crucicentrism (the centrality of the cross of Christ) are the defining evangelical beliefs and habits.[13] Those are essential evangelical characteristics, but biblicism, activism, and crucicentrism were also continuations of older Reformed emphases. For many evangelicals, however, the felt presence of the Holy Spirit was the major validation of conversion. Being born again in Christ and walking in the Spirit set them apart from their nominal Christian neighbors. The vast majority of white people in England and America considered themselves Christians, by virtue of their baptism and living in a society that was legally and culturally Christian. But for evangelicals, affiliation with "Christendom" did not make a person a true Christian.

The focus on the new birth and God's felt presence certainly applied to the evangelist George Whitefield. At the time of his conversion as an Oxford student in 1735, what seemed new to Whitefield was the joy, comfort, and guidance in the Holy Spirit. Through the influence of Charles and John Wesley (who were in the midst of their own journeys to conversion), Whitefield read a number of Pietist classics, including Arndt's *True Christianity*. But the most decisive book Whitefield read was *The Life of God in the Soul of Man* (1677) by the Scottish Episcopalian minister Henry Scougal. Scougal assured readers that "there is a new birth, and a divine inward operation of the Spirit of God which does constantly exert itself in the souls of the adopted sons of God." Before that point, Whitefield had seen obedience as the way to gain God's favor. But now he realized that he "must be a new creature." The evangelist recalled that he stood up with Scougal's book in his hand and said out loud, "Lord, if I am not a Christian, if I am not a real one, God, for Jesus Christ's sake, show me what Christianity is." "Real" Christianity was the consuming passion of evangelicals.[14]

In 1735 Whitefield broke through to the new birth, after long months of tortuous prayer and struggle. "The day-star arose in my heart," he wrote. "Now did the Spirit of God take possession of my soul." Scougal's promise of God's felt presence came true for Whitefield. In a 1736 diary now held at the British Library in London, Whitefield gave a daily account of walking in the Spirit. Over and over, he wrote of being "full of the Holy Ghost," often giving a specific amount of time that he was so filled. For instance, in March 1736 he wrote, "Joy in the Holy Ghost for 2 or 3 hours and illuminated in reading Scripture." As historian Bruce Hindmarsh has written, "The immediate sense of the Holy Spirit" drew together all of Whitefield's prior experiences "to light a fire and inspire an ardor of evangelical devotion in Whitefield, preparing him for the public ministry that was to come."[15]

And what a public ministry it was. Before long, crowds in the tens of thousands began to attend Whitefield's outdoor meetings in London. When he came to America in 1739 for his first tour, the crowds present at his assemblies sometimes exceeded the population of the town he was in. Whitefield's early ministry focused mostly on the new birth and the work of the Holy Spirit. Once he became more established and moderate, political affairs and the power of the British Empire increasingly blended with his message of the Savior's gospel. The blurring of power, politics, and gospel was a temptation even for the creators of the original evangelical template.[16]

Whitefield was the key English-speaking figure in the Great Awakening, an international series of revivals that stretched from Germany to Nova Scotia to the Caribbean. Although the greatest upsurge of the revivals transpired from about 1739 to 1742, events connected to the Great Awakening were already happening by the early 1730s and continued through the 1780s. In America, the revivals heavily influenced New England, New Jersey, and Pennsylvania first, and then swept into the southern colonies in the 1750s and 1760s.[17]

One of the most influential early revivals of the Great Awakening happened in 1734–35 in the Northampton, Massachusetts, church of the great theologian Jonathan Edwards. Edwards wrote about the revival in *A Faithful Narrative of the Surprising Work of God*. First published in London, *A Faithful Narrative* became the most famous description of a revival in Christian history, outside of the Bible's Book of Acts. Edwards explained that as the revival spread, "the Spirit of God began extraordinarily to set in, and wonderfully to work amongst us. . . . There was scarcely a single person in the town, either old or young, that was left unconcerned about the great things of the eternal world."[18]

The revivalists came under mounting attacks in the early 1740s, as critics said they were "enthusiasts" and troublemakers. Itinerant preachers barged into parishes and challenged the authority of established pastors, sometimes even suggesting that the local minister was unconverted. But Edwards defended the Great Awakening as, on balance, a work of the Holy Spirit. In *Religious Affections* (1746), arguably Edwards's greatest treatise, he contrasted those who were born again with those who were not. Only the former truly had the Holy Spirit. Only the converted could understand the things of God. "True saints only have that which is spiritual; others have nothing which is divine. . . . Natural [unconverted] men have not the Spirit; and Christ teaches the necessity of a new birth, or a being born of the Spirit, from this, that he that is born of the flesh, has only flesh, and no spirit (*John* 3:6). They have not the Spirit of God dwelling in them in any degree."[19]

Examples of the focus on conversion and the Holy Spirit could be multiplied many times over. Some moderate evangelicals were less comfortable with guidance from the Holy Spirit because it raised the specter of antinomian excess. Still, most eighteenth-century evangelicals thought of themselves as having a relationship with God through the Holy Spirit. Newport, Rhode Island's Sarah Osborn was one of the most prolific evangelical writers of late colonial New England. Although she was disposed toward moderation, in the 1760s she hosted a remarkable series of revivals at her house, eagerly attended by hundreds of blacks and whites. Several years before, Osborn had prayed that God would "give the Holy Spirit to those who ask him this day. This comprehends all other blessings. . . . O, come as on the day of Pentecost [Acts 2], and fill this room with thy glory and our hearts with thy praise."[20]

Edwards, Osborn, and Whitefield all embraced common beliefs of early Anglo-American evangelicals. But they also illustrated one of the basic problems of evangelicalism: the struggle over race and inequality, a problem that continues to mark evangelicalism today. Racial conflict and oppression have been enduring themes of American history generally, but evangelicals have an especially conflicted relationship to race. White evangelicals such as Edwards, Osborn, and Whitefield all wished to see African Americans come to faith in Christ. In a spiritual sense, they saw all people as equal before God because God had created all. Yet each of these figures also owned slaves.

Evangelical Christianity contains a powerful egalitarian impulse. The focus on individual salvation means that a slave might know God, while his or her master might be headed for hell. Such beliefs helped to precipitate the growth of the black church in the eighteenth and nineteenth centuries. But white evangelicals have often been reluctant to let their spiritual beliefs inform their views of racial oppression and inequality. Especially in the antebellum era, many white evangelicals used their beliefs to bolster slavery.

Edwards, Osborn, and Whitefield showed a range of responses to their slaves and the slave trade. Edwards owned a few
household slaves. He eagerly sought to include his slaves in his
revival meetings. He was critical of the abuses in the slave trade,
but he never came to believe that slavery itself was wrong.
A number of Edwards's successors, however, including his
son Jonathan Edwards Jr., would join the incipient antislavery
movement.[21]

In spite of their besetting poverty, Sarah Osborn's family
owned a slave boy named Bobey. In the early 1760s, Sarah
struggled with whether to sell Bobey. She clashed over the decision with Bobey's mother Phillis, who was a slave too but also
a sister in Christ. Osborn ultimately decided not to sell Bobey.
Later, Osborn was instrumental in the hiring of Samuel Hopkins
as pastor of her church in Newport. Hopkins became one of
revolutionary America's most ferocious critics of slavery.
Though we don't know for sure if her family ever freed Bobey,
Osborn did embrace antislavery principles under Hopkins's
influence. Late in life, she wrote:

Those we see here who once have been
Made slaves to man by horrid sin.
Now through rich grace in Christ are free,
Forever set at liberty.[22]

Osborn's wrestling over the morality of slavery contrasts
with Whitefield's growing acceptance of the institution. The
itinerant preacher showed some early concern about the treatment of slaves after he toured the southern colonies. He also
spoke regularly about educating slaves and welcomed Africans
and African Americans at his revival meetings. However,
wealthy plantation masters also experienced conversion under

his ministry, and by 1747 Whitefield had acquired a South Carolina plantation and became a slave owner.[23]

Whitefield then sought to legalize slavery in Georgia. The Georgia colony had originally banned the importation of slaves, but Whitefield and many other whites thought this law was ill conceived. Georgia would never flourish, Whitefield believed, until it had slave plantations like its neighbor South Carolina. He also hoped to use slave labor to fund the operations of his Bethesda orphanage outside of Savannah, which was the great charitable project of Whitefield's career. Unlike Edwards or Osborn, Whitefield became a proslavery activist. He was arguably the most influential voice in getting slavery legalized in Georgia in 1751.[24]

Whitefield was erratic when it came to his treatment of the marginalized people around him. Whitefield went out of his way, for instance, to assist Samson Occom, the leading Native American evangelical in eighteenth-century America. Whitefield hosted Occom when the latter came to England in the 1760s to raise money for Eleazar Wheelock's Indian charity school in Connecticut. Whitefield warned Occom not to trust Wheelock, his white onetime benefactor, and indeed when Occom came back with £12,000, Wheelock abandoned the Native American academy and instead founded Dartmouth College in New Hampshire, a school mainly for whites. Occom and Wheelock became permanently estranged because of the episode.[25]

In a more striking irony, Whitefield the proslavery activist helped to convert and inspire key African American evangelical leaders. One of these was Olaudah Equiano, who went on to become one of the most influential antislavery writers in the British Empire. Another was Phillis Wheatley, who was still a slave when Whitefield died on his last visit to America in 1770. We can only imagine the frustration and anger Wheatley might have felt, and mostly had to stifle, because of whites—including evangelicals—enslaving people like her. Some observers today would not include Wheatley as an evangelical, even though scholars of the eighteenth century commonly do so. Either way, we must acknowledge the stark differences in status and views of slavery between people like Whitefield and Wheatley. Yet the white family who owned her helped Wheatley, a talented writer, to publish a popular eulogy to Whitefield. She urged her fellow "Africans" to accept Whitefield's Jesus:

> Impartial Savior, is his title due;
> If you will choose to walk in grace's road,
> You shall be sons, and kings, and priests to God.

A variant edition of her poem was more blunt in its last line: "He'll make you free, and kings, and priests to God."[26]

In spite of Whitefield's support for slavery, his gospel message gave evangelical blacks—including slaves—hope for salvation and new resources with which to critique their oppressors. The original evangelical movement was multiracial. It remains multiracial today, even though many white evangelicals still take political and social stances that are dismaying to evangelical people of color.

At the outset, evangelicalism was basically a spiritual movement. The actions of its white leaders raised difficult questions about race, slavery, and other issues. Its limitations were many, but one would have to be quite cynical to view most eighteenth-century evangelicals as having, at root, political motivations for their revivalistic work. The typical early evangelical wanted to introduce all people—regardless of ethnicity or social standing—to the joys of salvation and the felt presence of God.

The original evangelicals were not primarily social or political reformers, partly because they remained a minority faction in Europe and America. Their lack of a reform agenda helped them to focus on eternal matters. But their individual, eternal emphasis also led some white evangelicals to turn a blind eye to manifest injustices around them, most notably the enslavement of African Americans. In some cases, white evangelicals such as Whitefield actively abetted the slave system. But black evangelicals and some of their white allies would find resources within their faith to make a moral argument for freedom.

2

Evangelicals Ascendant and the Coming of the Civil War

"Swearing Jack" Waller was a fast-living Virginia gentleman and lawyer, but he had a life-transforming encounter with Baptists in the 1760s. Waller came to believe their message about the threat of God's judgment and his need for forgiveness. He submitted his life to the lordship of Christ, and he received believer's baptism, the signature rite of the Baptists. Waller soon felt called to preach, but like dozens of other Baptist ministers in Virginia, Waller ran afoul of laws prohibiting preaching without a license. He first got arrested for disturbing the peace in 1768. (Other American colonists at that time were working to undermine the Townshend Acts, the latest in a series of provocative British tax laws.) The authorities' anger over Waller's preaching came to a head in 1771. A gang led by Caroline County's sheriff and a local Anglican parson dragged Waller out of a Baptist meeting. They whipped him until his blood ran free. Once the posse left, Waller cleaned himself up, went back to the meeting, and kept preaching. The Anglican "establishment" in Virginia was formidable, but evangelicals like Waller were indomitable. The surging evangelical faction vowed to bring down the establishment so that gospel-proclaimers like Waller could minister unfettered.[1]

The first great political campaign led by American evangelicals was the fight for religious liberty. This campaign was a reaction to governmental restrictions on evangelicals' ability to spread revival. Political advocacy was not a defining trait of early evangelicals. But they certainly engaged in politics, especially when governments kept them from doing what defined them: preaching the gospel.

Established churches were common in early modern Europe and the New World colonies. Some were quite rigid; others offered latitude for dissent. But they all gave official sanction to Christianity, and usually to one favored denomination. Establishments reflected the pervasive assumption that religion was so valuable in society that it deserved governmental support. But beginning with Anabaptists in Europe, some Christian dissenters questioned the validity of establishments. They argued that established churches inevitably became corrupt and persecuted true believers.

In the 1630s, the Puritans brought a relatively harsh form of religious establishment to Massachusetts and Connecticut. It is a myth that the Puritans wanted "religious freedom." They were seeking to freely practice biblical Christianity, but they did not tolerate dissent. In this context, Roger Williams was the most articulate defender of religious liberty and church-state separation in early America. A former Puritan minister, Williams criticized colonial Massachusetts for its mingling of government and church. Williams argued that true believers were to be separated from the world. Anticipating Thomas Jefferson's famous phrase of a century and a half later, Williams contended that God had erected a "wall of separation between the garden of the church and the wilderness of the world."[2] Williams earned banishment from Massachusetts for airing his views, and he became the founder of the Rhode Island colony, the English colony that mandated the clearest separation between church and state.

Massachusetts had the toughest policy against dissent. Typically, the colony just banished dissenters such as Williams and Anne Hutchinson. But Massachusetts also hanged four Quaker missionaries between 1659 and 1661. (These Quakers had first been banished and told not to return, but they did so anyway.) Massachusetts passed a host of laws banning Quakers, Baptists, and other undesirable groups.[3] The Puritans were hardly alone in their intolerant ways. Many English colonies had laws restricting Catholics and Jews. Since most Muslims in colonial America were African slaves, their religion did not generate much specific notice in early American laws.

Many prominent revivalists of the Great Awakening were members of established churches. George Whitefield was an Anglican minister based in England, where the Church of England was (and is) the official denomination. Jonathan Edwards was a Congregationalist, the established church in the New England colonies (except in Williams's Rhode Island). But some of these established ministers got into trouble during the Great Awakening, as they flouted rules about parish boundaries. The most notorious evangelist of the era was James Davenport, a Congregationalist graduate of Yale College. His flamboyant behavior and the unruly crowds he attracted led Connecticut to pass anti-itinerancy statutes against him. The colony wanted to stop Davenport and other evangelists from preaching in churches without the resident pastor's permission. Connecticut's campaign against Davenport culminated in a wild confrontation at the Hartford courthouse in 1742 when the colonial militia dispersed his followers. Davenport was not finished, though. Connecticut banished him, but he returned in 1743, holding a book and clothes burning in New London. When Davenport pitched his own pants on the bonfire, his embarrassed followers stopped the display. The humiliated Davenport turned to moderation, seeking to redeem his damaged reputation.[4]

The Great Awakening also produced dissenters who broke away or "separated" from the established churches. The Separates created new congregations that were committed to revival. Some of these Separates became Baptists, who were often the most fractious dissenters. (Roger Williams was briefly a Baptist.) Baptists in America in the 1600s were marginal and often despised. Because of the Great Awakening, however, the Baptist movement was itself reborn. Especially in New England, some evangelicals revisited the traditional practice of infant baptism. Not seeing any explicit scriptural justification for infant baptism, they argued that strict conformity to the Bible required the practice of believer's baptism alone. To many observers, refusing to baptize infants jeopardized the eternal destiny of children and hacked at the fabric of a Christian society, which depended upon infant baptism.

Baptists were also aggressive proselytizers. Baptists sent missionaries from New England to the South in the 1750s. This began a massive transformation of the South from America's most unchurched region into the nation's Bible Belt, a change that was well under way by the Civil War.

Separates and Baptists were ardent advocates of religious liberty. Calls for religious freedom drew inspiration from English philosopher John Locke, who argued that government should never coerce religious belief. The government's authority extended only to actions that affected civil peace and safety. This distinction between civil and spiritual affairs influenced founders such as Thomas Jefferson and James Madison as well as the evangelical dissenters.

Virginia's Jefferson and Madison would become some of the dissenters' most powerful allies, even though these political leaders did not embrace evangelical doctrine. In the years leading up to the Revolution, Virginia authorities had imprisoned dozens of renegade preachers such as Swearing Jack Waller. Once the Revolution broke out, Jefferson, Madison, and the evangelicals saw an opening for full religious freedom. Patriot authorities had a war to fight against Britain, and they could not afford to alienate fellow Americans over differences in religion. Officials stopped jailing Baptist preachers, but that was not enough for the evangelicals. They wanted Virginia to stop playing favorites in religion altogether.

After the Continental Congress adopted the Declaration of Independence, evangelicals in Virginia clamored for the disestablishment of the Anglican Church. The Baptists and other activists submitted a "Ten Thousand Name" petition to the Virginia assembly calling for an end to Anglican religious taxes, so that every "yoke may be broken and that the oppressed may go free." Jefferson called the debate over Virginia's established church one of the "severest" in his political career. In late 1776, Virginia legislators granted exemptions to Baptists and other dissenters who did not wish to pay taxes to the Church of England (soon to be renamed the Episcopal Church in America).[5]

When the war ended, Virginia had to decide whether to keep a church establishment. Some traditional Christians, such as popular governor Patrick Henry, wanted to create a "general assessment" for religion. Under that system, Christians would pay religious taxes, but they could designate the church to receive their contributions. The general assessment would have stopped requiring people to support churches they did not attend. But for the evangelical dissenters, and for Madison and Jefferson, this was still insufficient. Baptists condemned the general assessment as "repugnant to the spirit of the gospel," noting that Jesus did not use coercion to further his cause. They wanted no one to have to act against the dictates of conscience. Evangelicals flooded the assembly again with petitions calling for full religious liberty. The resistance scuttled Henry's plan. Madison reintroduced the Bill for Establishing Religious Freedom, which Jefferson had originally proposed in 1779. Jefferson was away in Paris in 1786, so Madison got the bill passed in his absence. Jefferson's statute affirmed a remarkably modern relationship between church and state, prohibiting taxes for religion and dispensing with civil penalties for unorthodox religious belief.

Baptists were similarly wary of the Federal Constitution of 1787 because of its initial failure to stipulate protections for religious liberty. In 1789, Madison assured Virginia Baptists that he planned to sponsor a religious freedom amendment to the Constitution when the first Congress met. He kept his word. The First Amendment's religion clauses prohibited Congress from making any law "respecting an establishment of religion" and guaranteed Americans the "free exercise of religion."[6]

The First Amendment was a great victory for evangelicals and for Jefferson and Madison. But it inaugurated an enduring struggle to define disestablishment in America. As white evangelicals became politically powerful, they have sometimes pursued cultural and legal establishment in ways that purist evangelicals of the founding era would have disdained. The temptations of political and cultural power have been strong for white evangelicals. Many evangelicals sought to bring their moral convictions into the public square, in causes from antislavery to prohibiting

Sunday mail. In the 1810s and 1820s some sought to end mail delivery on Sundays, which they regarded as a profanation of the Sabbath. Many Baptists criticized the campaign, however, saying that the government should not require Sabbath observance. The Baptist layman, U.S. senator, and future vice president Richard M. Johnson of Kentucky insisted that Congress was not "a proper tribunal to determine what are the laws of God." As a general rule, evangelicals have been at their best when using their political sway to defend the weak and oppressed (such as slaves), rather than seeking to impose evangelical practices, ideas, or standards of conscience on the public (such as in the Sunday mail controversy). But the line between those two modes of advocacy is often blurred. Proslavery Christians, for example, insisted that antislavery evangelicals should just let Americans act according to their conscience with regard to slave owning, rather than impose their antislavery values on everyone else. Abolitionists countered that slavery was utterly wrong and should have no sanction in American law.[7]

These types of issues illustrate the enduring evangelical challenge to achieve the proper relationship between faith and government. Evangelicals today often balk at "separation of church and state" because of the stringent way that courts have applied the doctrine over the past half century. But evangelicals were largely responsible for church-state separation in the founding era, working with nonevangelicals such as Thomas Jefferson and James Madison to establish religious freedom.

Evangelicals were split in their view of Thomas Jefferson when he won the presidency in 1800. Some saw him as a heretic and unbeliever. Others—especially Baptists—knew about his less than orthodox views, but supported him as a champion of religious liberty. Baptist evangelicals' fondness for Jefferson led to one of the oddest events in the history of the American presidency. On New Year's Day in 1802, the Baptist evangelist John Leland presented Jefferson with a twelve-hundred-pound block of cheese, the "mammoth cheese," as newspapers called it. The gift came from Leland's Baptist haven of Cheshire, Massachusetts. That Sunday, Leland also preached a sermon before Congress and the president. One Federalist member of Congress scoffed at the "cheesemonger" Leland, calling the Baptist minister a "poor, ignorant, illiterate, clownish preacher." Jefferson had cast himself as a man of the people, and Federalist opponents cast his evangelical supporters as clowns.[8]

Leland represents an intriguing evangelical stance in American politics, one that has largely become extinct today. Leland enthusiastically supported nonevangelical presidents such as Jefferson and Andrew Jackson *because* they wanted to maintain a clear distinction between church and state. Leland was so radically opposed to Christian establishments that he even registered doubts about the propriety of government-paid chaplains.[9] As we shall see, many American evangelicals in the decades since Leland—and especially since World War II—have supported nonevangelical politicians who promised to *promote* Christian cultural and legal establishment. They have especially looked for political allies to help them combat threats such as atheistic communism, court decisions against religion in public schools, and a secularizing American society. Leland was such a thoroughgoing evangelical that Christian social influence through politics mattered little to him. With memories of government persecution fresh in his mind, what Leland wanted more than anything was to freely preach the gospel of the new birth.

New Year's 1802 was a big weekend for religious liberty at the presidential mansion. In addition to accepting the mammoth cheese, Jefferson sent a public reply to the Danbury

Baptist Association of Connecticut, which had congratulated him on his election and urged him to keep defending religious freedom. Jefferson viewed his letter to the Danbury Baptists as an opportunity for "sowing useful truths & principles among the people." Among those truths was that Jefferson was no anti-Christian zealot, in spite of what his Federalist rivals charged. Unlike George Washington and John Adams, Jefferson was not inclined to call for national days of prayer and fasting, but he was not opposed to holding religious services in government buildings, as illustrated by Leland's sermon.[10]

Jefferson's letter to the Danbury Baptists has taken on a prominent role in the annals of church-state relations. Jefferson wrote that "religion is a matter which lies solely between man and his God, . . . that the legitimate powers of government reach actions only, and not opinions, I contemplate with sovereign reverence the act of the whole American people which declared that their legislature should 'make no law respecting an establishment of religion, or prohibiting the free exercise thereof.'" According to him, the religion clauses of the First Amendment built a "wall of separation between church and state."[11]

Many evangelicals in 1802 would have agreed, seeing the wall of separation as a guard against government coercion in religion. Other evangelicals, however, still supported some forms of government sanction of religion. For example, evangelicals and other Christians assumed that government-run schools would promote a generic brand of Protestantism. Thus, many were dismayed in the 1960s when the Supreme Court ruled that school-sponsored prayer and Bible reading violated the First Amendment's establishment clause. In *Engel v. Vitale* (1962), a major Supreme Court case on school prayer, Justice Hugo Black contended that official prayer "breaches the constitutional wall of separation between Church and State." Black was an Alabaman and a former member of the Ku Klux Klan whose strict separationist views were connected to his anti-Catholic animus.[12]

Evangelical support (and that of Americans generally) for prayer in public schools has remained strong in the twenty-first century. But evangelicals today talk about the issue less than they did in the 1970s and 1980s. It is not always clear whether people responding to pollsters' questions about school prayer are affirming the right of individuals to pray or official school sponsorship of prayer. Evangelical leaders such as apologetics writer Os Guinness and historian Mark Noll have argued that the formal prayers sponsored by public schools are hardly worth fighting for. Recent school prayer advocacy by evangelicals has centered on student-led devotions such as "See You at the Pole." This annual event encourages students to meet at the flagpole before school to pray, and it avoids many church-state complications.[13]

In the early 1800s, critics of disestablishment expected the absence of state churches to engender moral decline. Advocates for religious liberty such as James Madison and John Leland, however, argued that separating denominations from the state would purify Christian faith in America. The First Amendment initially prohibited only a national establishment. States could maintain official churches, and many did so. Establishment on the state level ended finally with Massachusetts dropping direct support for the Congregationalist Church in 1833. In the meantime, America had witnessed another massive series of revivals, typically called the Second Great Awakening. Episodes such as the Cane Ridge Revival in Kentucky in 1801 fueled the Second Great Awakening. But just as important were the labors of evangelical ministers—especially Baptists and Methodists—who preached to settlers on the trans-Appalachian frontier, in the Ohio River Valley, and in Gulf Coast territories stretching out to Texas.

Frontier church planting made evangelicalism the default religion in much of the growing United States. By the eve of the Civil War, America had come as close numerically to being a "Christian nation" as it had ever been, at least in terms of numbers.[14] Whether it was a Christian nation in substance is doubtful, given the harsh realities of slavery, Native American removal from the Southeast, and other glaring moral problems.

Although the revivals fueled evangelical growth in the first half of the nineteenth century, the Second Great Awakening is more a term of convenience than precise reality. Revivals associated with this awakening lasted from the 1790s to the 1830s. The Second Great Awakening perpetuated trends from the First Great Awakening, including the emphasis on the new birth in Christ and the work of the Spirit. The new revivals proceeded in a national context of religious freedom and disestablishment, however. Churches and ministers were obligated to compete for adherents as never before.

Another key difference between the first and second awakenings was that many revivalists of the 1800s emphasized a person's free will to accept Christ. In the First Great Awakening, most revivalists were Calvinists. Following the Reformed tradition, Calvinists believed that God had to change the will before a person could respond to Christ's offer of forgiveness. They also taught that Christ had died only for God's "elect," while Arminians insisted that Christ had died for all people. England's First Great Awakening was more influenced by Arminian or free-will theology than America's was. Free-will theology was a hallmark of John Wesley's Methodists, who became a major factor in America after the American Revolution. A significant Calvinist strain lingered among American evangelicals, but free-will theology better matched the cultural mood of postrevolutionary America, obsessed as it was with liberty.

Charles Finney, whose preaching in the North anchored the later phases of the Second Great Awakening, insisted that no one should wait passively for conversion or revival, as if they were inaccessible mysteries. Sinners should choose to follow Christ, and believers should choose to experience revival. Because of the nation's near-deification of freedom (at least freedom for whites), Finney's Arminianism was a more natural fit in antebellum America than the Calvinism of Whitefield, Edwards, and Sarah Osborn.[15]

The Second Great Awakening also featured a strong leveling impulse. Converts filled with the Holy Spirit found themselves speaking in public settings where they ordinarily could not. At the Cane Ridge Revival, a seven-year-old girl exhorted a crowd while sitting on a man's shoulders until, exhausted, she slumped over on his head. When an old man near her called her a "poor thing," the girl's head snapped up: "Don't call me poor, for Christ is my brother, God my father, and I have a kingdom to inherit, therefore don't call me poor, for I am rich in the blood of the Lamb," she proclaimed.[16]

Likewise, at an 1802 North Carolina revival, a "negro-woman" attended initially to mock her penitent friends. But upon hearing the threat of God's wrath, she fell into a "state of horror and despair" for hours, crying out, "O hell! hell! hell! Thy pangs have seized me!" Echoing images from Jonathan Edwards's "Sinners in the Hands of an Angry God," the African American woman said that "she saw hell-flames below, herself hung over by a thread, and a sharp, bright sword drawn to cut it through." Soon she broke through to conversion and began shouting "Glory, glory!"[17]

Small numbers of Native Americans experienced conversion during the Second Great Awakening. One was the Methodist Pequot William Apess, among the best-known advocates for Native American rights in antebellum America. He reveled in the Methodist doctrine of general atonement, or the idea that Christ died for all. To Apess, this meant that Native Americans benefited from God's mercy. "Christ died for all mankind . . . age, sect, color, country, or situation made no difference," he wrote. In his autobiography (the first one published by a Native American author), Apess attributed the revivals, his conversion, and his call to ministry to the work of the Holy Spirit. "The Lord moved upon my heart in a peculiarly powerful manner," he recalled, "and by it I was led to believe that I was called to preach the gospel of our Lord and Savior Jesus Christ. . . . We read in the Bible that in former days, holy men spoke as they were moved by the Holy Ghost. I think this is right." Apess initially doubted whether he, a "poor ignorant Indian," was fit to preach. But God confirmed his calling by divine signs and dreams. Soon he became a trenchant critic of white Christians' treatment of Native Americans and African Americans. Apess illustrated evangelical social and political advocacy at its best, as he employed his Christian fervor to champion the dignity of the most oppressed people in the U.S.[18]

Critics highlighted the frenzied and exotic aspects of the Second Great Awakening in order to discredit it. Methodist churches were growing fast and, at least in the early 1800s, they heavily emphasized the discernible movements of the Spirit. The Restorationists (Churches of Christ), a denomination also growing quickly during the period, were one group that preferred more rationalistic and strictly biblicist religion. Although their roots were evangelical, the Churches of Christ were becoming more sectarian and exclusive. They vociferously criticized

the Methodists. One Restorationist writer said that the Methodists' traveling Circuit Riders were like "fiery, swift-winged com-
ets, erratic in their course." When they summoned penitents to
the altar, Methodists opened the "fireworks of hell" to generate
an emotional response. The Methodist audience "jumped and
yelled, and barked, groaned and grunted, howled and screamed,
cried and laughed." This Restorationist writer exclaimed, "Oh
Religion! what follies are not perpetrated in thy name?"[19]

Some evangelicals were more comfortable with outward
manifestations of the Spirit than others. New England Congregationalists insisted that "stillness" could as easily mark true
revival as noise. But ecstatic experiences and the felt presence
of the Spirit appeared even among the soberest evangelicals of
the Second Great Awakening. The Calvinist Congregationalist
Edward Dorr Griffin presided over a revival in Newark, New
Jersey, in 1806–7. Griffin was just the sort of evangelical who
might have been skeptical of "enthusiasm." Yet he matter-of-
factly reported that God sowed the seeds of the Newark revival by sending revelatory dreams. For those affected by these
reveries, "days of dissipation were separated by nights, in which
fancy would bear the sinner to the bar of God, and fill him with
terrors of the final judgment." The Newark revival drew hundreds of converts of all ages and races, he said, "including
drunkards, apostates, infidels, and those who were lately ma-
lignant opposers."[20] Griffin would become the first pastor of
Boston's Park Street Church (a historically influential evangelical congregation) and the president of Williams College,
traditionally seen as the birthplace of the American overseas
missionary movement.

The Second Great Awakening saw a massive national outburst
of organizing for evangelism. American evangelicals had earlier

endorsed the concept of missions, or going to distant lands in order to bring the gospel to unevangelized peoples, but they did not make systematic efforts to encourage missions until the Second Great Awakening. Most missions before 1810 were informal efforts and not called "missions" per se. Informal missions (then and now) often entailed the movement of congregants and pastors, such as the Methodist Circuit Riders, into frontier regions. Christian immigrants and travelers created new churches as they went. An organized American missionary effort first developed out of a powerful prayer meeting at Williams College in 1806. Students there dedicated their lives to sharing the gospel in far-flung countries. This led to the creation in 1810 of the American Board of Commissioners for Foreign Missions (ABCFM), the most prominent evangelical missionary agency in the nineteenth century. The ABCFM's missions were global, reaching from Hawaii to China and from the Middle East to the lands of Native Americans. In the early 1800s, then, American evangelicalism adopted a fully international profile, a characteristic that would become more pronounced over time.[21]

ABCFM leaders represented the faction of antebellum evangelicals that historian Sam Haselby has labeled "national evangelism." This cohort, led mostly by northeastern "gentry and capitalists," was committed to evangelism and to inculcating civilization, education, and moral reform. These evangelicals especially sought to reform uncouth whites who were aligned with the "frontier revivalism" of Baptists, Methodists, and other sectarian evangelical groups.[22]

Some frontier evangelicals, such as the Primitive Baptists, opposed missionary societies like the ABCFM. Frontier evangelicals saw these agencies as unbiblical and run by money-grubbing Yankee elites. Nevertheless, organizations such as the ABCFM and the American Baptist Missionary Union flourished during the first half of the 1800s. The ABCFM's work connected evangelism to moral reform, demonstrated in episodes such as its opposition to President Andrew Jackson's Indian removal campaign in the 1820s and 1830s. This confrontation led to the Supreme Court case of *Worcester v. Georgia* (1832). The plaintiff in this case, ABCFM missionary Samuel Worcester, had been arrested for residing in Cherokee territory without a state license. *Worcester v. Georgia* affirmed the Cherokees' territorial sovereignty, but the state of Georgia and Andrew Jackson effectively ignored it. In the founding era and antebellum period, evangelicals found that they could not restrict themselves just to evangelism, missions, and building up churches. Their beliefs and missionary work often led to political engagement and moral reform, including advocacy for Native Americans and slaves.[23]

To evangelicals, missions also entailed distributing Bibles, books, and gospel tracts. In the 1740s, George Whitefield had set the pattern for evangelical printing and for much of the American print trade in general. Aided by entrepreneurial publishers such as Ben Franklin, Whitefield's popularity led to a huge expansion of print in Britain and America between 1739 and 1741. In the colonies, total publications rose 85 percent during those three years, with most of the increase attributable to material by or about Whitefield (including attacks on him). He pioneered the evangelical penchant for current media technologies from cheap print to the internet. Evangelical culture has always been connected to books and other publications, and more recently to music, films, online content, and more. Nonevangelical entrepreneurs such as Franklin have often been key players in shaping evangelical media culture, even if these entrepreneurs cared more about profits and politics than saving souls.[24]

George Whitefield was a publishing phenomenon, but the evangelical print trade did not reach maturity until the early 1800s. Not coincidentally, the broader American print industry also flourished during these years. Total book and periodical production in America increased 500 percent during the second quarter of the nineteenth century. The Methodist Book Concern, opened in 1789, was the first systematic evangelical book publisher in the U.S. Many other denominational and interdenominational outlets followed, including the American Bible Society (1816), the American Sunday School Union (1817), and the American Tract Society (1825). In 1855, these three big interdenominational publishing ministries sold about 2.4 million volumes total. This accounted for about 16 percent of all books published in America that year. These groups often sold Bibles and other publications at discounted rates, seeking to reach as many people as possible. They assumed that people would value the Bible more if they bought it, however, rather than just receiving a free copy. (Free Bible distribution by evangelicals became more common with the rise of groups such as the Gideons, founded in 1899.) Evangelicals believed in using books and other media formats to convey godly, biblical words. When animated by the Holy Spirit, such media would do evangelistic work even when no missionary was present.[25]

While the Bible has remained America's perennial bestselling book, evangelical-themed titles such as Harriet Beecher Stowe's *Uncle Tom's Cabin* (1852) and Rick Warren's *The Purpose Driven Life* (2002) have routinely topped yearly best-seller lists. Early religious trade publishers such as Harper & Brothers (founded 1818) often found their biggest sales in titles that could reach both core evangelical readers and a broader audience. Harper & Brothers scored its greatest success of the late nineteenth century with Lew Wallace's *Ben-Hur: A Tale of the Christ* (1880), which sold four hundred thousand copies in nine years, surpassing *Uncle Tom's Cabin* in popularity. In spite of many evangelicals' early hesitancy about the morality of movies, Hollywood returned repeatedly to the Ben-Hur story in hopes of attracting both devout and secular viewers. They enjoyed a massive hit with the 1959 version of the movie starring Charlton Heston. The spheres of secular and evangelical media have often overlapped.[26]

For evangelicals, the distribution of religious literature was evangelistic but it also had reforming functions. If the republic were to survive, most leaders believed, Americans needed to remain rooted in the great traditions of Anglo-American law, the ancient Greek and Roman republics, and Christian history, including the Bible. This desire led to a flowering of secondary and collegiate education in antebellum America. The new colleges were typically affiliated with Protestant denominations.

Most colleges before the Civil War still catered only to white men. The evangelical Oberlin College in Ohio, which opened in 1833, was unusual in its commitment to both a co-ed and a multiethnic student body. Charles Finney would join the faculty at Oberlin, a center of midwestern antislavery activism and a stopover for escaped slaves on the Underground Railroad. Mount Holyoke Female Seminary became the first women's college in America when it opened in Massachusetts in 1837. Its founder, Mary Lyon, was a devotee of the "New Divinity" theology of Jonathan Edwards's successors. The New Divinity was a great engine of evangelical benevolence. Lyon saw women's education as having overtly evangelical purposes. In particular, she envisioned Mount Holyoke training female schoolteachers who would then evangelize schoolchildren. Partly because of this sort of impulse, the U.S.—and especially New England—achieved unusually high levels of female literacy.[27]

Aside from evangelism, missions, and education, evangelicals spearheaded moral reform causes such as crusades against poverty and alcohol abuse. The heyday of both urban ministry and the temperance campaigns lay in the future, but the decades before the Civil War saw major evangelical mobilization on both issues. Temperance might seem like a typical evangelical instance of moralistic meddling. But evangelicals and other temperance proponents were responding to a serious social problem that was more rampant in antebellum America than it is today. The average American drank at least three times more alcohol in the early 1800s than in modern America. Those who drank to excess also often struggled with health problems, domestic violence, or unemployment. Lyman Beecher, Presbyterian pastor and patriarch of the Beecher clan of American Christian leaders (which included his daughter Harriet Beecher Stowe), helped to found the American Temperance Society in 1826.[28]

Evangelicals had addressed the needs of the poor dating back to Whitefield's Bethesda orphanage in Georgia. New missionary societies in the 1800s preached the gospel to the urban poor and provided them with material assistance. The early Sunday school movement in America and Britain gave special attention to impoverished children, believing that biblical education could bring both salvation and an improved station in this life. Phoebe Palmer, a key Methodist leader, established the Five Points mission in New York City in 1850, anticipating a host of similar missionary works initiated after the Civil War. Palmer's Five Points mission focused mainly on evangelism and education, but it also offered shelter for the homeless and abused. Prior to the late nineteenth century, most evangelical ministries to the poor prioritized proselytizing over material relief. But some form of ministry to impoverished people has always been a hallmark evangelical concern.[29]

Palmer was a key evangelist in a major revival that swept through Britain, eastern Canada, and America in 1857–58. The revival coincided with a financial cataclysm that generated urgent spiritual interest among North America's businessmen. The 1857–58 revival is often called the Businessmen's Revival or the Prayer Meeting Revival for its professional-led devotional assemblies. Palmer viewed the revival as an outpouring of the Holy Spirit for mass conversion. She also believed that God's blessing on her speaking ministry confirmed the promise of Joel 2:28 that "your sons and your daughters shall prophesy." Palmer asked, "Was this promise of the Father as truly made to the daughters of the Lord Almighty as to his sons?"[30] Women's roles in the church would remain controversial, and both male and female evangelicals commonly accepted biblical injunctions that seemed to place limitations on women's ministerial roles. Traditional Christian prohibitions on women clergy never fully excluded exhorters, Bible teachers, and evangelists such as Palmer, however.

Whatever their concerns about women in ministry or work among the poor, in antebellum America no issue was more divisive for evangelicals than slavery. African Americans who were becoming evangelical Christians—especially in Methodist and Baptist churches—did not equivocate over slavery. They knew slavery was wrong, but they typically had little opportunity to espouse that opinion before whites. The revolutionary era saw occasional bursts of black Christian challenges to slavery, however, including one by the poet Phillis Wheatley, who called slave masters "modern Egyptians" in a 1774 letter. That same year, the governor of Massachusetts received a petition from Christian slaves asking for freedom. Citing Galatians 6:2, they asked, "How can the master be said to bear my burden when he bears me down with the heavy chains of slavery and oppression?" When masters permitted slaves to attend church, it was typically in white-pastored congregations. Free blacks had more latitude to form their own churches, especially in northern cities. The African Methodist Episcopal (AME) denomination was founded in 1816, led by the former slaves Richard Allen of Philadelphia and Daniel Coker of Baltimore.[31]

African American evangelicals also engaged in missions. Daniel Coker went with the American Colonization Society in 1820 to establish an AME congregation in Sierra Leone, West Africa, where he lived the rest of his life. The African American Baptist pastor Lott Cary of Richmond, Virginia, founded the African Baptist Missionary Society in 1815. (A white Baptist formally served as the head of the society in order to allay racist concerns about Cary.) In 1821, Cary went to Liberia in West Africa, establishing a Baptist congregation in Liberia's capital, Monrovia. In 1828 Cary became governor of the colony.[32]

By the antebellum period, white evangelicals in the South had largely assuaged other whites' worries about evangelizing slaves. Making slaves Christians would render them better slaves, the evangelicals said. Nevertheless, hostile whites routinely blamed slave revolts on reckless evangelical preachers who proclaimed God's love and liberty for all people. South Carolina whites lashed out at Charleston's AME congregation in the wake of an alleged 1822 revolt by Denmark Vesey, who was one of the founders of the church. Vesey was executed, and the church was demolished. Virginia's white authorities likewise saw Nat Turner's revolt in 1831 as a product of Turner's visionary spirituality. (Turner was a lay Baptist preacher.) Critics complained about Baptist evangelists in the South who spouted "ranting cant about equality" among the slaves.[33]

Around the same time as Turner's revolt, growing numbers of whites and blacks in the North began arguing that slavery was against God's will. As with religious liberty, evangelicals

heavily influenced the antislavery cause. Antislavery was another notable instance of black and white evangelicals entering
the public square on behalf of oppressed people. British evangelicals led by William Wilberforce and other moral reformers
of the "Clapham Sect" achieved their greatest victory in 1833
when Britain abolished slavery in its empire. American antislavery reformers wanted the U.S. to follow suit. Some abolitionists
were skeptics and religious liberals, but many were evangelicals,
such as the merchant-philanthropists Lewis and Arthur Tappan.
Evangelical operators on the Underground Railroad included
Harriet Tubman and the Methodist exhorter and educator
Laura Haviland.[34] In a more radical vein, evangelical convictions
inspired Nat Turner and John Brown (who led an attack on the
federal arsenal at Harpers Ferry, Virginia, in 1859) to use violence against the "Slave Power" of the white South.

   Prior to the Civil War, however, the vast majority of white
southern evangelicals were proslavery. Or at least they consigned the slavery issue to the realm of politics, not church.
Many northern evangelicals were also silent on the issue. This
reticence frustrated abolitionists such as the prominent African
American writer Frederick Douglass. For example, Douglass
regarded the Mexican War of the late 1840s as a craven attempt
by southern masters to expand U.S. territory in the Southwest
for more slave plantations. Thus he considered the war immoral and un-Christian. "What say our evangelical clergy to
this blasphemy?" Douglass asked in 1848. "That clergy seem as
silent as the grave; and their silence is the greatest sanction to
the crime."[35] White evangelical silence regarding concerns of
people of color is a central component of today's evangelical
crisis, but such passivity has a long history.

   For evangelicals, the key issue in the slavery debate was
understanding what the Bible taught on the matter—but the

Bible was not entirely clear about the morality of chattel slavery. Its authors seemed to accept forms of slavery that existed in the ancient Hebrew and Roman worlds. A "plain reading" of Scripture, which evangelicals preferred, supported the proslavery side because the Bible nowhere condemned slavery outright. But antislavery evangelicals thought that the spirit of the Bible and Jesus's teachings ("Do unto others as you would have them do unto you") could never sanction chattel slavery and its associated abuses.[36] Enslaved African Americans intimately knew the pain, fear, and oppression of slavery. Many slaves believed that the same God who had freed Israel from Egyptian slavery would free them too. Pro- and antislavery pastors thundered out anathemas against one another for failing to obey what they saw as the Bible's teaching on the slave question. This just made the divisions between evangelicals more bitter. As Abraham Lincoln reminded Americans in his Second Inaugural Address, "Both [sides] read the same Bible and pray to the same God." Yet that common Christian confession could not avert the Civil War.

By the 1840s, evangelical doctrine and style dominated major Protestant denominations, especially the Baptists and Methodists. Both these denominations split in the mid-1840s over the slavery issue. In each case, members could not agree whether someone holding an official church position could also be a slaveholder. (Presbyterians had split earlier, partly over divisions related to revivalism. The New School and Old School Presbyterians would both divide again on the eve of the Civil War into pro- and antislavery wings.) As the Methodist Church splintered, one leader warned that if the denomination could not hold together, it would finally pit "brother in the Church against brother, and the north against the south—and when thus arrayed . . . civil war and far-reaching desolation must be the final results."[37] In 1861, this remarkable prophecy came true.

3

The "Fundamentalists" and Evangelical Controversy

Evangelicals would never regain the level of national cohesion they possessed before the national Methodist and Baptist denominations broke into sectional factions in the 1840s. For many American Christians who were already disturbed by the antebellum rancor over slavery, the Civil War shook their confidence even more deeply. Horrified by the defeat of the Confederate army, a young South Carolinian named Grace Brown Elmore wrote, "I know not how to bear it. I cannot be resigned. Hard thoughts against my God will arise, questions of His justice and mercy refuse to be silenced."[1]

Evangelicals had experienced many divisions before the 1840s, such as those between Calvinists and Arminians, between the forces of "national evangelism" and "frontier revivalism," and between opponents and defenders of slavery. In the decades preceding the Civil War, white evangelicals separated bitterly into northern and southern camps. Most of those splits persisted long after the war. Baptists would never reunite nationally. Northern and southern white-led Methodists would not reunite until 1939. By that time the Methodists had aligned denominationally with mainline (nonevangelical) Protestants, in spite of an enduring evangelical presence within American Methodism that continues today. (As a popular descriptor of major Protestant denominations, the term *mainline* began to appear by the early 1960s.)[2]

Divisions between white and black churches further separated evangelicals. The formation of countless independent black churches and denominations after the Civil War allowed African American Christians to create institutions free from white supremacy. The reassertion of white supremacy after the war was signaled by the rise of racist groups such as the Ku Klux Klan. In addition to mass departures from the Southern Baptist Convention, most African Americans left the Methodist Episcopal Church, South, after the Civil War. From 1865 onward, African Americans' institutional connections to white-led evangelical denominations and ministries became tenuous. This is one reason why African Americans often do not identify as evangelicals, even when their doctrine and experiences seem characteristically evangelical. In recent years, pollsters have regularly employed "evangelical" as a category that does not apply to blacks anyway.

In addition to ethnic and regional divisions, the half century after the Civil War would see evangelicals—especially white northern evangelicals—embroiled in wars against theological liberalism. This would change American evangelicals' primary cultural stance. Founded in the mid-1700s as a reaction against nominal Christianity, evangelicalism was becoming a movement arrayed against theological liberalism by the turn of the twentieth century. For a time, "fundamentalist" would effectively become a synonym for evangelical. Fundamentalists battled against theological modernists and their seemingly novel views of the Bible's authority and historicity.

The fundamentalists' conflicts would take them once again into realms of politics and law. In the 1910s, evolution was just one concern in the fundamentalist repertoire. Christian politician William Jennings Bryan's emergence as a fundamentalist champion helped to redefine evolution as *the* fundamentalist issue of the 1920s. Bryan and his followers campaigned to ban the teaching of evolution in public schools. To most fundamentalists, Darwinian evolution raised difficulties about humankind's place in creation, and its teaching challenged the de facto Protestant establishment's control of public schools.

The fundamentalist-modernist controversy began as an intra-Protestant fight over seminaries and churches; it turned into a clash over control of government-run schools. Evangelical beliefs have always had political applications. But as we have seen, evangelicals have been most faithful to their tradition when protesting against manifest injustices like slavery rather than trying to impose a de facto or de jure establishment. Attempts to ban Sunday mail delivery, the sale of alcohol, and the teaching of evolution all reflected that establishmentarian impulse. This impulse has routinely taken evangelicals away from their dissenting roots. Well-meaning (or crassly opportunistic) politicians have often led rank-and-file evangelicals into such establishmentarian efforts. Some of those politicians (such as Bryan) have been evangelicals, some not. But the establishmentarian crusade of the early 1920s culminated in Bryan's sensational collapse at the 1925 Scopes "Monkey Trial." Promoting anti-evolution laws was one of the most misguided evangelical ventures ever because it focused so much energy on mandating a particular Christian view of science in public schools. The

Scopes Trial was a major precedent for the crisis of politicization that bedevils evangelical Christians today.

Even as the spectacular feuds over theology unfolded, evangelical congregations grew during the Gilded Age and Progressive Era. Rising independent African American denominations founded innumerable new churches, mission agencies, and educational institutions in the aftermath of the Civil War. In 1895, African American leaders joined in Atlanta to create the National Baptist Convention of the USA, which by 1906 had more than 2.2 million members.[3]

The late 1800s also saw the beginnings of Asian evangelical communities in the West, with new Asian-pastored Protestant congregations in Seattle and San Francisco. The Baptist evangelist Fung Seung Nam ministered to the burgeoning Chinese population of San Francisco in the early 1870s, preaching outdoors in Chinese to crowds that numbered in the thousands. A report urged that the Northern Baptist denomination erect a church structure for mission work among San Francisco's Chinese people. If it did so, "nearly a thousand heathen could be gathered within its walls every Sunday." Hispanic evangelical groups also began to appear in the American Southwest during this period. Hispanic culture was dominated by Catholicism, but Methodists, Baptists, and other Protestant groups began sending missionaries into Texas and New Mexico after the Civil War. San Antonio saw the founding of the Primera Iglesia Bautista Mexicana in 1887, Texas's first enduring Hispanic Baptist congregation.[4]

The Methodist missionaries Thomas and Emily Harwood went to New Mexico in 1869, inaugurating a mission among Spanish-speaking people that would last for four decades. Typical of their time, the Harwoods saw the Hispanic population of New

Mexico as religiously and culturally backward. But they still trained Hispanics as exhorters and preachers. As a general rule, Christian movements have done better at reaching people when the evangelistic appeal came from members of the same ethnic group. That was the case in New Mexico, as the Hispanic preachers the Harwoods recruited spawned a network of Spanish-speaking Methodist churches. One of the Hispanic Methodist ministers, Leandro Fernandez of the El Paso District, commended Thomas Harwood for his commitment to the "great and noblest of causes, that is, the saving of souls by the help of the Redeemer, the Lord Jesus Christ." In a swipe at the original Spanish colonizers of New Mexico, Fernandez praised Methodists for seeking to save souls without the use of "arms, only faith in the Lord Jesus." By 1900, the Methodists had fifty-eight churches in New Mexico alone, with more than fifteen hundred members total.[5]

The most celebrated American evangelist of the Gilded Age was Dwight Moody. Originally a Chicago shoe salesman, Moody participated in the Businessmen's Revival of 1857–58 and the Young Men's Christian Association (YMCA) when he was a young man. Along with the Young Women's Christian Association, the YMCA became a key evangelical parachurch organization in Britain and America. The YMCA in Chicago sought to attract "the idle and thoughtless young men of the city" to evangelize them and extend the moral influence of the city's churches. (The leadership of the YMCA would go in a modernist direction by the 1920s, and by the 1970s it had abandoned explicitly Christian aims.) The frenetic Moody started a popular Chicago Sunday school that eventually morphed into a church Moody pastored. In the 1870s he preached at packed meetings in Britain, and by the time he came back to the U.S. in 1875 he was a full-fledged celebrity.[6]

Moody's preaching focused on conversion. Moody trumpeted the "Three Rs": "ruin by sin, redemption by Christ, and regeneration by the Holy Ghost." In spite of his involvement with the socially minded YMCA, Moody was skeptical about Christian reform causes. Drawing on popular "premillennial" beliefs about the end times, Moody suggested that the apocalypse and the return of Christ to earth were imminent. He sought to rescue as many sinners as he could before the end came.[7]

Moody also wrote extensively about the empowering work of the Holy Spirit for "success." Moody's focus on successful living accorded with self-improvement manuals dating back to Ben Franklin's autobiography. Unlike the worldly-wise Franklin, Moody insisted that power for victory in the Christian life came through the Holy Spirit. Here Moody was echoing teachings of Phoebe Palmer and of devotional writer Hannah Whitall Smith's popular 1875 book *The Christian's Secret of a Happy Life*. Smith emphasized that the "indwelling Holy Ghost is the possession of even the weakest and most failing child of God." Many Christians did not appreciate the Spirit's power, Smith noted, and they needed to "submit fully to His possession and His control." Smith and her husband were key figures in well-known conferences on holiness and the Christian life hosted in Keswick, England. These meetings drew as many as ten thousand attendees by the early twentieth century. The Keswick conferences have remained seminal evangelical assemblies to the present day, with major British and American speakers at Keswick including the Anglican minister John Stott and the evangelist Billy Graham.[8]

Like Smith, Moody insisted that Christians could not overcome sin, understand the Bible, or effectively share their faith without the Holy Spirit's leading. In his book *Secret Power; or, The Secret of Success in Christian Life and Christian Work*,

Moody maintained, "The Gospel has not lost its power. . . . We don't want any new doctrine. It is still the old Gospel with the old power, the Holy Ghost power."[9] Other well-known evangelicals promoted this "higher-life" theology, including the prolific R. A. Torrey, author of works such as *The Baptism with the Holy Spirit* (1895). Torrey, a Yale Divinity School graduate, served as the head of the Moody Bible Institute and the Bible Institute of Los Angeles as well as pastor of Chicago's Moody Church and Los Angeles's Church of the Open Door.

The ideal of the higher life and the sanctifying work of the Spirit also attracted African American evangelicals. The former slave Amanda Berry Smith imbibed higher-life principles through her friendship with Hannah Whitall Smith and the writings of Phoebe Palmer. Amanda Berry Smith went on to become a missionary in the British Isles, India, and Liberia. She also influenced Charles H. Mason, who taught about the higher life and the work of the Spirit in African American Baptist churches in the South prior to founding the Church of God in Christ in Mississippi in 1897. Mason would become a Pentecostal at the 1906 Azusa Street Revival in Los Angeles, which saw an epoch-making outbreak of speaking in tongues. As we have seen, Pentecostals typically teach that the baptism of the Holy Spirit happens after conversion. For Pentecostals, the baptism of the Spirit is marked by speaking in tongues. This ecstatic speech is understood either as a divine language or as a foreign language that the speaker does not know. The Church of God in Christ would become the nation's largest black-led Pentecostal denomination. Early white Pentecostals mostly became affiliated with the Assemblies of God, founded in Arkansas in 1914.[10]

The widespread emphasis on the Holy Spirit extended even to leaders who became associated with theological modernism.[11]

The broad-based fascination with the Spirit in the age of Moody shows that evangelicals were relatively unified around the importance of the Spirit's ministry before Azusa Street. Many evangelical leaders did believe that the Spirit's extraordinary gifts, such as instantaneous healings and speaking in tongues, had ceased with the end of the apostolic era of church history. But evangelicals were not yet split into the well-defined hostile camps over the work of the Spirit that would emerge with the coming of the Pentecostal movement in the early 1900s.

Moody's view of the Holy Spirit influenced many evangelicals of the era. These included Emma Dryer, who in the 1880s would found (with Moody's encouragement) a Bible school that was a forerunner to Chicago's Moody Bible Institute. Dryer and Moody also illustrated the growing evangelical penchant for entrepreneurial parachurch ministry. Evangelicals had been engaged in such pragmatic work at least since George Whitefield opened his Bethesda orphanage in Georgia. The great reform, missionary, and Bible societies that began in the early 1800s were parachurch operations, partnering with supportive churches. But until Moody, no evangelical leader had been quite so disconnected from a denomination. He partnered with many denominations but committed to none. Moody and associates like Dryer funneled resources into areas of practical need: evangelism, Bible training, conferences, schools, and more. These priorities resulted in Dryer's "Chicago Bible Work," Moody's schools for boys and girls in Northfield, Massachusetts, and popular summer Bible conferences. Moody's evangelical agencies and events depended on his brand rather than a denominational connection. The legacy of Moody's entrepreneurial, nondenominational style has made evangelicalism nimble and nonbureaucratic. At times it has also given the movement an ahistorical mindset, a penchant for the flashy, and a lack of institutional ballast and accountability.[12]

Moody and his song leader Ira Sankey also helped to foster the evangelical use of popular music, a trend pioneered by prolific songwriting Methodists such as Charles Wesley in the 1700s. Moody and Sankey turned Christian music into big business. Sankey began producing editions of his gospel music hymnal in 1873, and it was a runaway success. More than 50 million copies of *Gospel Hymns and Sacred Songs* had been sold by 1900. Sankey's hymns drew on the vernacular of African American spirituals, though without the spirituals' prophetic edge regarding the suffering of slaves. More refined ministers scoffed at the emotionalism of Sankey's collection. Its poignancy was illustrated by the New York Baptist Annie Hawks's hymn "I Need Thee Every Hour" (1872):

> I need Thee ev'ry hour,
> Most gracious Lord;
> No tender voice like Thine
> Can peace afford.
> I need Thee, oh! I need Thee;
> Ev'ry hour I need Thee;
> O bless me now, my Saviour!
> I come to Thee.

"I Need Thee Every Hour" continues to appeal to many Christian worshippers (not just evangelicals), even as worship bands today accompany the song with drums and electric guitars. In its original context, the hymn was also an example of how evangelicals such as Hawks, Sankey, and Moody repackaged key themes—such as conversion and walking with God—into the vocabulary of new generations. Such hymns remind us that evangelicals are a singing people.[13]

As seen in Amanda Berry Smith's global ministry, evangelicals' commitment to the "higher life" in the Spirit spawned many missionary careers. Many evangelical women, who typically could not gain ordination as pastors, found their ministry niche as missionaries. The Southern Baptist Lottie Moon was among the most celebrated missionaries of the era. She went to China in 1872, laboring there for forty years. As she ministered among Chinese women and children, Moon struggled with loneliness and depression, and she sought comfort in the felt presence of the divine. In the mid-1880s Moon asked for prayer for "the outpouring of the Holy Spirit . . . that I may be clothed with power from on high by the indwelling of the Spirit in my heart."[14] Lottie Moon remains a heroic figure in Southern Baptist circles today. The denomination's annual Lottie Moon Christmas Offering for missions has routinely raised more than $150 million in recent years.

The 1880s and 1890s saw a surge in British and American missionaries, whose number increased from fewer than a thousand to almost five thousand between 1890 and 1900. In America, a critical transition came at a student missionary conference at Moody's Mount Hermon School in Massachusetts, where ninety-nine students committed to foreign missionary service. By 1888, this Student Volunteer Movement (SVM), led by the Methodist John R. Mott, had added thousands more students to lists of those volunteering for missionary work. The Presbyterian missions leader A. T. Pierson popularized the "watchword" of the SVM, which was "the evangelization of the world in this generation." SVM leaders believed that the Kingdom of God was comprised of people from every "tribe, tongue, and nation," as suggested in the Book of Revelation. Thus, they held that believers must evangelize the lost in "unreached" places before the return of Christ. The Presbyterian missions leader Robert Speer declared to the SVM that "what we are doing will hasten the coming of that radiant morning when the eastern skies shall be full of the glory of his coming [Matthew 24:27]."[15]

Critics argued that missionary activity was a pretext for American and British imperialism. Many of the SVM's leaders did assume that Anglo-American civilization was superior, and that the rest of the world needed to adopt Western culture. The SVM's rise also coincided with imperial developments such as America fighting in Cuba and the Philippines during the Spanish-American War (1898). Missionary advocates were tempted to develop a dependent, uncritical relationship with British and American colonial powers. Republican politicians heralded the missionary movement as a part of extending American influence around the world. Senator Albert Beveridge, an Indiana Methodist, proclaimed, "Of all our race [God] has marked the American people as His chosen nation to finally lead in the regeneration of the world. This is the divine mission of America." Initially there was not much difference between many evangelicals and their modernist rivals on questions of missions, civilization, and empire. By the 1920s and 1930s, however, fundamentalists and modernists disagreed over the merits of "converting" people on the foreign mission field. Increasingly, modernists believed that missionaries should be agents of Christian service and Western civilization, not conversion.[16]

Missionary advocacy helped to sustain long-standing connections among American, Canadian, and British evangelicals. Leaders from Britain and North America dominated the landmark World Missionary Conference in Edinburgh in 1910, with only seventeen non-Western delegates present out of a total of twelve hundred. (There were also about six to eight African American delegates.) Engagement with missions gave many evangelicals familiarity with foreign cultures and peoples. Missionary reports, such as Lottie Moon's letters home from China, were widely circulated in evangelical congregations. Some overseas missionaries also became scholarly experts and diplomatic figures connected to their chosen mission field. Samuel Zwemer, who joined the SVM at Hope College in Michigan, became the most prolific and influential American evangelical writer on Islam and the Middle East in the first half of the twentieth century. Zwemer served as a missionary in Arabia and elsewhere in the Middle East before joining the faculty at Princeton Theological Seminary.[17]

Evangelicals remained engaged with domestic and international politics during the late nineteenth and early twentieth centuries. White evangelicals widely supported the campaign to prohibit the sale of alcohol. The Methodist Frances Willard helped turn the Woman's Christian Temperance Union into the largest women's organization in America by the 1890s, with 150,000 members. Willard testified that she had experienced sanctification, or freedom from sin, at a Phoebe Palmer revival in 1866. Although Willard was trending toward a more liberal, inclusivist theology, in the late 1800s she worked with Dwight Moody in revivals and temperance advocacy. Willard also urged Christians to aid persecuted Christians around the world. She especially spoke out on behalf of the Armenian community in Turkey, which suffered genocidal attacks from Turks in episodes from the 1890s to the 1910s.[18]

Evangelical opinion on issues like prohibition was never uniform. J. Gresham Machen, a Presbyterian theologian at

Princeton and astute Christian commentator, did not support prohibition. Machen was a social drinker and saw no scriptural ban on Christians consuming alcohol in moderation. Many African American evangelicals supported prohibition as a means of social "uplift" and respectability. However, other African Americans were more concerned about issues such as lynching and black disenfranchisement. Although the Fifteenth Amendment to the Constitution had guaranteed color-blind voting rights, southern white politicians undermined blacks' ability to vote, sometimes in the name of prohibition. "Drys" used stereotypes of drunk, lascivious black men in order to stoke prohibitionist sentiment. Thus, some African Americans partnered with "wet" advocacy groups because the wets helped blacks preserve their voting rights.[19]

An epidemic of lynching in the South from the 1890s to the 1910s was the most extreme example of how American whites sought to silence and intimidate blacks after emancipation. Thousands of lynchings occurred, the majority of them targeting southern blacks. African American leaders such as Walter White of the National Association for the Advancement of Colored People (NAACP) contended that white churches shared blame for the grotesque violence. "Evangelical Christian denominations have done much towards creation of the particular fanaticism which finds an outlet in lynching," he wrote. Many white evangelicals expressed concern over lynching. But they typically lamented the lawlessness of such acts more than the racial hatred they reflected. Lynchings typically took place after a black man was accused of a crime, such as the rape or murder of a white person. A Southern Baptist resolution in 1906 reflected the equivocation of white evangelicals about lynching, saying that "lynching blunts the public conscience, undermines the foundations on which society stands, and if unchecked will bring on anarchy." But, the resolution went on, "our condemnation is due with equal emphasis, and in many cases with much greater emphasis, against the horrible crimes which cause the lynchings."[20]

Equivocation sometimes turned into outright endorsement of lynching by white evangelicals. Some even participated in the lynchings, and untold numbers of white evangelicals joined groups such as the Ku Klux Klan. (The Klan also attracted a wider range of active and nominal Protestants.) Some observers have even noted troubling resemblances between the rituals of lynchings and those of evangelical revival meetings. For example, it was not unusual for the mobs to give the accused an opportunity to repent, confess, or pray before execution. A few white evangelicals engaged in anti-lynching activism, including William Northen, a Confederate soldier, governor of Georgia, and Southern Baptist leader. After Atlanta's horrific 1906 race riot, Northen helped to form the biracial Business Men's Gospel Union, which sought to build a network of Christian anti-lynching activists. But even Northen made it clear that he was disgusted with "second class" blacks and whites who were often behind both the crimes and the vigilantism that lay at the heart of lynching. He fondly recalled the ostensibly placid social order of the antebellum South. Stopping lynching would not undermine white supremacy or lead to racial integration, Northen assured white audiences.[21]

Equivocation about lynching was standard for white evangelicals, especially in the South. Sam Jones, a Methodist preacher and the era's best-known southern evangelist, illustrated the failure of white evangelicals to speak lucidly on the topic. When a black laborer named Sam Hose was castrated and burned to death in Georgia in 1899, Jones originally expressed concern. (Hose was accused of murdering his boss, a white farmer, and raping his wife. Subsequent investigations suggested that Hose had acted in self-defense in the killing, and that he had not committed sexual assault.) But Jones later approved of the lynching: "The man, white or black, who commits an outrage on a virtuous woman, deserves death. Sam Hose deserved to be burnt."[22]

Some black churches may have been ambivalent about prohibition, but they were not ambivalent about lynching. They vociferously condemned it and participated in anti-lynching efforts led by the NAACP and activists such as the writer Ida B. Wells. Wells was especially tough on evangelical leaders such as Moody and Frances Willard, who equivocated about lynching or downplayed the issue. Wells observed, "Our American Christians are too busy saving the souls of white Christians from burning in hellfire to save the lives of black ones from present burning in fires kindled by white Christians." Black church leaders such as the Baptist Nannie Helen Burroughs and the Methodist Mary McLeod Bethune (who attended Moody Bible Institute) boosted NAACP campaigns for federal laws against lynching. Likewise, in 1921 the *National Baptist Voice* publicized the NAACP's attempt to get pastors to take a special Sunday to preach on the theme "Justice to the Negro—the Test of Christianity in America." The newspaper contended that in light of its racial violence and oppression, the U.S. represented "the archsinner among the nations, and its protestations of democracy are as sounding brass or a tinkling cymbal [I Corinthians 13:1]." White evangelicals' vacillations about lynching caused deeper divisions between black and white Christians who otherwise shared similar evangelical convictions. The epidemic of lynching, and the churches' varied responses to it, was emblematic of the political and social divides between black and white conservative Protestants over the past century.[23]

Evangelicalism was at heart a movement about biblical doctrine, the salvation of sinners, and the work of revival. But that spiritual focus could also become one of the chief excuses white evangelicals used to justify their silence on severe injustices such as lynching. Of course, white evangelicals did get involved in political issues such as prohibition. White supremacists insisted, however, that all evangelicals should remain quiet about lynching, or at least remain equivocal. In 1897, a Georgia newspaper reviled several Atlanta preachers who "seem to have run entirely out of gospel subjects to preach on. Last Sunday several of them preached against lynching, and not one of them preached against [black] rape."[24] Whether an evangelical regarded a sermon topic as unduly "political" depended a great deal on his or her ethnicity and social standing.

White fundamentalists were more likely to condemn booze or liberal theology than lynching. (Most white modernists were not eager to address racial violence, either.) The threat posed by modernist thought to traditional Christian beliefs was not new to the post–Civil War period. Leading evangelists of the Great Awakening had routinely spoken against Deism, an enlightened system of religious thought that questioned the reliability of the Bible. Deism influenced a number of American founders, including Ben Franklin, Thomas Jefferson, and Tom Paine. Paine's popular *Age of Reason* (1794) launched a caustic attack on traditional Christianity and the Bible.

By the Civil War era, evangelical churches had become so dominant that they represented a de facto religious establishment in many areas. This established status made the rise of modernist thinking seem like more of a threat. One aspect of modernist thought, the theory of evolution, caused a sensation upon the publication of Charles Darwin's *On the Origin of*

Species (1859). But conservative Christians were not unified in their response to evolution. Some rejected the theory as inherently godless, while others believed that evolution could complement the biblical account of creation. Others, such as theologians Charles Hodge and B. B. Warfield of Princeton Theological Seminary, argued that evolution caused problems only when it functioned as a theory regarding the origins of life, especially of humankind. To the extent that evolutionary theory removed God from that creative process, it was unacceptable to traditional Christians.

Many evangelical/fundamentalist leaders were initially more concerned about "higher criticism" of the Bible than evolution. For decades, some European scholars had historicized the Bible and its miraculous claims. Some argued that the Bible's stories stood in the same literary category as myths of ancient Greece and Rome. The Bible's stories might be morally instructive, but they did not convey facts, the higher critics maintained. Most important, higher critics such as the French historian Ernest Renan, author of *The Life of Jesus* (1863), challenged the notion that Jesus worked miracles or was divine. Those scholars looking for a historical Jesus often found merely a human Jewish reformer, not the Son of God.

To evangelicals, doubting the divinity of Christ put a person's eternal fate in jeopardy. To them, higher critics undermined the Bible's trustworthiness and the idea that Jesus was the unique and divine Savior. This was not a simple disagreement over theological technicalities. To conservative theologians such as J. Gresham Machen, modernism represented a *different religion* from Christianity. Machen declared, "The great redemptive religion which has always been known as Christianity is battling against a totally diverse type of religious belief, which is only the more destructive of the Christian faith because it makes use of traditional Christian terminology. This modern non-redemptive religion is called 'modernism' or 'liberalism.'"[25]

Seminaries and religious colleges stood at the forefront of controversies over evolution and higher criticism. In some denominations, such as the Northern Methodist Church, modernist thought took hold among leading theologians without much debate. In other denominations, such as the Methodist Episcopal Church, South, and the Southern Baptist Convention, modernist thought made little headway. Those denominations successfully marginalized early adopters of modernist thought.

For example, in 1879 the Southern Baptist Theological Seminary (Louisville) secured the resignation of Crawford Toy, a professor of Hebrew. Toy questioned the traditional Mosaic authorship of the Pentateuch (the first five books of the Hebrew Bible) and the idea that the prophetic Book of Isaiah was written by just one person. Toy suggested that when New Testament authors claimed Hebrew Bible verses for prophetic purposes, they were taking those verses out of context. When Toy left Southern Seminary, he took a position at Harvard and eventually became a Unitarian (someone who believes in the unity of God alone, and not the Trinity). Toy was once romantically involved with Baptist missionary Lottie Moon, but they broke off their engagement, perhaps due in part to Toy's unorthodox beliefs.[26]

In perhaps the most sensational clash over modernism, the Presbyterian Church in 1892 disciplined Charles Augustus Briggs, a professor at New York's Union Theological Seminary. Briggs advanced theories about the Hebrew Bible that were similar to Toy's. Indeed, Toy and Briggs had been students together in Berlin. Toy told Briggs that he was "glad to find that we are in accord as to the spirit of Old Testament study, and rejoice that you have spoken so earnestly and vigorously on behalf of the spirit of broad, free, spiritual minded investigation. . . . It will require patient and wise effort to dislodge the traditional narrowness that has obtained so firm a foothold in some quarters."[27]

Fundamentalists warned that if the seminaries were captured by modernists, liberal thought would infect up-and-coming pastors and go out to laypeople. The Baptist A. J. Frost sounded the alarm in 1886 when he warned that "a thousand pulpits are drifting from the doctrine of inspiration [of the Bible], the deity of Christ, the vicarious atonement, the resurrection of the body, and the eternal retribution."[28]

The fundamentalist movement attempted to codify non-negotiable evangelical doctrines ("fundamentals") in the face of the modernist challenge. Rejection of the theory of evolution was not yet one of those core doctrines. Instead, as suggested by Frost's warning, the fundamentals focused on five biblical concerns: the "inerrancy" and perfection of Scripture, Jesus's virgin birth, Christ's death as the payment (atonement) for sins, Christ's bodily resurrection from the dead, and the veracity of the Bible's miracles. Although traditional Christians had always affirmed Scripture's divine inspiration, the doctrine of inerrancy countered the notion that the Bible contained errors of fact, chronology, or science.[29] Some key fundamentalists, including J. Gresham Machen, largely avoided the subject of evolution, believing that Christians should focus instead on defending time-honored theological precepts. Machen followed his older Princeton Seminary colleague B. B. Warfield in contending that as a scientific matter, evolution did not necessarily contradict Scripture.[30]

Some fundamentalists believed that the doctrine of inerrancy did require opposition to evolution. They insisted that evolution contradicted God's immediate creation of Adam and

Eve in Genesis. Some fundamentalists would add other doctrines to the list of fundamentals as well, such as the belief in the pre-millennial, imminent return of Christ. The premillennial (that is, before the thousand-year millennial reign of God's Kingdom) return of Christ was a key feature of "dispensational" theology as taught in resources such as the enduringly popular study Bible by C. I. Scofield. But in the twelve-volume series *The Fundamentals* (1910–15), theologians and pastors tended to focus just on the five main points of fundamentalism. The authors marshaled their best arguments against the modernists in favor of traditional Protestant doctrine. They affirmed scientific learning, but only if it did not rule out God's role in the created order. Several of these fundamentalist writers were open to evolution, assuming that God was still the first agent behind creation.[31]

Fundamentalism took a new turn when William Jennings Bryan helped make the movement virtually *equal* to opposing evolution in public schools. Bryan grew up with deep evangelical influences in Baptist, Methodist, and Presbyterian churches of Illinois, his home state. He became one of the greatest orators in American political history, and the most influential Democratic politician in the 1890s and early 1900s, running three times as the party's presidential nominee and serving as secretary of state under Woodrow Wilson. He had little connection to the emerging fundamentalist movement, however, until he left the Wilson administration. Bryan then found himself adrift politically. He rediscovered his calling in the anti-evolution campaign. Believing that the earth was very old, Bryan did not hold to a literal reading of the "days" of creation in Genesis 1. (Formal "young earth" theory, as articulated by evangelical advocates of creation science, only started to become popular in the 1960s.) But Bryan rejected the idea that humans developed from lower forms of life over long periods of time.[32]

Bryan began his barnstorming attacks on evolution in 1920. Within a couple of years, he had gained notoriety and was receiving news coverage as a fundamentalist. Many theological conservatives were enamored with his prominence. In spite of his lack of theological training, Bryan was almost elected the national moderator of the Northern Presbyterian Church in 1923.[33]

Bryan and other fundamentalists became convinced that America's public schools were indoctrinating young people with evolutionary theory. In an explosion of evangelical establishmentarianism, some fundamentalists—especially in the South—began pushing state legislatures to ban instruction on evolution. Pastors such as the Baptist J. Frank Norris of Fort Worth, Texas, sought to recruit Bryan to campaign for anti-evolution legislation in their states. Norris and others ignored traditional Baptist hesitancy about trying to make government units serve the church. Instead, the anti-evolutionists employed arguments based on the right of a political majority to impose its will, in the name of preserving America's Christian heritage. Tennessee Baptist pastor O. L. Hailey wrote, "Evangelical Christians, . . . who constitute the majority of the citizens of the United States, have a right to object . . . to the teaching of anything in the schools which are supported by the state, which is contrary to the doctrines taught in the Bible."[34]

The clash over evolution came to a head in 1925, when Tennessee passed a law against teaching evolution. John Scopes, a science teacher in Dayton, Tennessee, agreed to violate the law, and his trial turned into one of the biggest media spectacles in American history. Virtually everyone involved with the trial, including Bryan, wanted it to become a journalistic extravaganza.[35] Evangelicals have often used the latest media to spread the word about the gospel, but media coverage has also routinely taken evangelicals into unexpected territory. This happened in 1925 when Bryan battled against the liberal lawyer Clarence Darrow, who represented Scopes for the American Civil Liberties Union. The trial became a farce when Bryan took the stand in defense of the Bible. In exchanges eagerly reported by the national media, Darrow stumped Bryan with simple questions regarding the historicity of the Bible and its miracles. Only days after the trial concluded, Bryan died. Ever since, the trial and Bryan's death have symbolically marked the end of the fundamentalist movement.

The actual history of fundamentalism after Scopes was not so tidy. Scopes was initially convicted, since he had obviously broken the law, and fundamentalists did not see the trial as a defeat for the anti-evolution cause. But fundamentalists after Scopes became stereotyped as buffoonish southern bumpkins. The sharp-witted journalist H. L. Mencken savaged Bryan and his southern supporters as "gaping primates from the upland valleys." (Mencken much preferred J. Gresham Machen, whom he praised as "a man of great learning and dignity.") The popular play and movie *Inherit the Wind*, loosely based on the episode, did more to shape average Americans' impressions of Scopes, Bryan, and fundamentalism than did the actual trial. When the movie came out in 1960, the popular image of fundamentalism became more deeply connected to Bryan, who had been dead for thirty-five years.[36]

Fundamentalism had begun as an attempt to combat theological modernism in the church and seminaries. Bryan, a Christian politician with little connection to the fundamentalist movement, had transformed fundamentalism—in image, if not in practice—into a movement to ban the teaching of evolution in government schools. The New York Baptist Curtis Lee Laws, who coined the term *fundamentalism*, was one of dozens of evangelical leaders who had a better claim to fundamentalist leadership prior to Bryan's tragic flameout in Dayton. Laws ruefully noted, "Mr. Bryan was never the leader of fundamentalism except that his prominence caused the papers to count him the leader."[37] The Scopes Trial illustrated the temptations of media access, establishmentarian politics, and celebrity politicians in evangelical history. That combination of power politics and media imagery accounts for much of the crisis evangelicals are facing today.

4

The Neo-Evangelical Movement and Billy Graham

After the Scopes Trial, American evangelicalism in its contemporary form began to coalesce. Conservatives had largely failed in their efforts to bar modernists from major denominations and seminaries, especially in the North. J. Gresham Machen left Princeton in 1929 to form Westminster Theological Seminary in Philadelphia. In 1936, Machen also helped to found the Orthodox Presbyterian Church (OPC), a denominational alternative to the mainline Presbyterian Church in the USA (PCUSA). Not all evangelicals left mainline churches and seminaries, of course. For example, prominent Pittsburgh Theological Seminary professor John Gerstner stayed in the PCUSA from the 1950s through the 1980s, seeking to maintain evangelical influence even as his denomination headed in a modernist direction. But in forming Westminster and the OPC, Machen illustrated one of the key habits of fundamentalists: separating from theological modernists when they could not be defeated in the existing denominations and seminaries. After the Scopes Trial, "fundamentalist" became closely associated with this separatist inclination.[1]

"Evangelicals" took a different path than fundamentalists did. Even during the fundamentalist-modernist wars, many evangelicals (especially those associated with Dwight Moody) focused on evangelism, missions, and higher-life piety more than theological combat. After Scopes, conservative Protestants began to disagree among themselves about the merit of partnering with organizations that included theological liberals. Fundamentalists insisted that they would not cooperate with theological liberals, or even cooperate with theological conservatives who *associated* with modernists. Some observers today use *fundamentalist* and *evangelical* as synonymous terms, but doing so is incorrect. One way to tell the difference is to ask whether the conservative Protestant in question approved of Billy Graham, who cooperated with modernists and Catholics. If conservative Protestants admired Graham, they were probably evangelicals; if not, they were likely fundamentalists.

By the early 1940s, a number of evangelical leaders worked to move beyond fundamentalism to craft an intellectually robust, culturally engaged form of conservative Protestantism. These neo-evangelicals remained concerned about modernism, but they also partnered with diverse Christian groups in order to present the gospel in a forceful yet winsome way. The signal moment in this remolding of evangelicalism was the founding of the National Association of Evangelicals (NAE) in 1942. The NAE offered an alternative to the modernist Federal Council of Churches as well as to the fundamentalist American Council of Christian Churches.

Harold John Ockenga, the president of the NAE and pastor of Boston's Park Street Church, still warned of what he called the "terrible octopus of liberalism." But Ockenga believed that broad evangelical unity was essential to combating the modernist menace. This meant that the NAE would be open to a broad range of churches, agencies, and individuals, and the organization did not insist upon pristine separation from modernists. The new evangelicals realized that many conservatives remained in the mainline denominations. They believed that denominations were less important than the spiritual unity among true believers in Christ. The NAE also was willing to cooperate with Pentecostals, including the Assemblies of God. The cofounder of the NAE, J. Elwin Wright, was deeply influenced by Pentecostal revivalism. Although fundamentalists reviled the Pentecostals' practices of faith healing and speaking in tongues, NAE leaders were amenable to partnering with Pentecostals in spite of differences. With his vision of unity among theological conservatives, Ockenga proclaimed, "The day has dawned and the hour has struck inaugurating a new era in evangelical Christianity."[2]

Of course, no interdenominational agency by itself could inaugurate a new religious era. But the NAE reflected an energetic post-fundamentalist vision for evangelicals. It also signaled more sophisticated political engagement, as the NAE opened a lobbying office in Washington. Evangelicals in the 1940s wished to maintain radio and television broadcasting rights, as the Federal Council of Churches was pressuring the major networks to eliminate conservative religious programs. The NAE's growing political savvy would lead to some successes for conservative Protestants, but it would also contribute to the emerging evangelical crisis of politicization.[3]

The most conspicuous deficiency of the NAE was the failure of its white leaders to include African Americans and other nonwhites. Racial tension was also a major component in the evangelical crisis. This component of the evangelical predicament had deep historical roots, dating back to George Whitefield's proslavery advocacy. The NAE erected no formal barriers for blacks to join, but neither did its leaders do much to address problems of race, not wishing to alienate segregationists in their midst. Frustrated by the lack of attention to civil rights, a group of African American NAE members founded the National Black (originally "Negro") Evangelical Association (NBEA) in 1963. NBEA members included evangelicals with connections to institutions such as Wheaton College in Chicago and Fuller Theological Seminary in Pasadena, California. Pentecostals also played a central role in the NBEA. The most influential Pentecostal leader in the early NBEA was Fuller Seminary graduate William H. Bentley, who served as NBEA president from 1970 to 1976, and as president of the United Pentecostal Council of the Assemblies of God (a largely African American and Afro-Caribbean denomination) from 1981 to 1989.[4]

The founding of the NAE heralded new estrangement between fundamentalists and evangelicals, but the relationship between Pentecostals and "cessationists" in evangelical circles was more complex. After all, belief in the discernible work of the Holy Spirit was a signature of the historic evangelical movement. But Pentecostals and charismatics expected more immediate and dramatic manifestations of the Spirit than many evangelicals found palatable. Speaking in tongues was the distinctive feature of Pentecostal piety, and tongues made many evangelicals uneasy.

The era of the Scopes Trial also saw the emergence of a powerful Pentecostal movement, especially among Latinos and African Americans. Methodists, Presbyterians, and other Protestants had started missionary work among Latinos in the Southwest, but during the twentieth century the growth in Latin American Protestantism was mostly Pentecostal and charismatic. Much of that Latino Pentecostal advancement was connected to the Azusa Street Revival in Los Angeles in 1906. Pentecostals typically did best among Latinos when they gave Latino ministers the authority to preach.

One of the most powerful Latino Pentecostal evangelists and faith healers of the early twentieth century was the Mexican-born Francisco Olazábal. Admirers compared Olazábal favorably to Billy Sunday, the flamboyant white evangelist. Olazábal's mother had served as a lay Methodist preacher, heavily influencing her son's ministry. Olazábal studied at a Methodist seminary in Mexico before becoming a pastor in El Paso, Texas, in 1911. Then, after studying briefly at Chicago's Moody Bible Institute, Olazábal served as an itinerant preacher in California.[5]

Olazábal encountered California Pentecostals who had been part of the Azusa Street Revival, and he became a Pentecostal himself. In 1918, he received ordination as an Assemblies of God pastor. Soon Olazábal returned to El Paso, which for centuries had been a main transit point for people journeying through northern Mexico and the American Southwest. In 1919–20, Olazábal saw a major outbreak of revival in El Paso. "God is using divine healing to bring many souls to Christ," he wrote. Olazábal reported that some four hundred to five hundred Mexicans had accepted Christ, far exceeding the number of Mexican converts that other El Paso Protestants had seen in recent years. Many also prayed to receive the baptism of the Holy Spirit. Olazábal left the Assemblies of God in 1923 over tensions with white leaders. Before his death in 1937, Olazábal held titanic revivals in Chicago, New York City, Mexico, and Puerto Rico.[6]

Olazábal also preached at joint services in Los Angeles with Aimee Semple McPherson, the best-known white Pentecostal evangelist of the era. As a Pentecostal, a female preacher, and a divorcée, McPherson was controversial, to say the least. Her Angelus Temple in Los Angeles sat five thousand people, and she reached millions more with her radio ministry. McPherson downplayed provocative aspects of Pentecostalism, especially speaking in tongues. But her ministry remained distinctly charismatic. The title of her popular book *This Is That* was taken from Acts 2: "This is that which was spoken by the prophet Joel; 'And it shall come to pass in the last days, saith God, I will pour out of my Spirit upon all flesh: and your sons and your daughters shall prophesy.'" In the final section of the book, a stenographer supplied a list of "visions, prophecies, messages in tongues and interpretation given by Sister McPherson." The book claimed that she gave the messages when "she was completely under the power of the Holy Spirit." The collection noted that she gave these "as though speaking in tongues," but unlike most instances of tongues, "they came in English." She also built bridges to the broader fundamentalist community of the 1920s by teaching on the end times, denouncing theological modernism, and hosting William Jennings Bryan to speak on evolution.[7]

McPherson also touted American patriotism, a favorite theme of many Pentecostals and evangelicals. "Christianity and patriotism go hand in hand," she said. "One must be loyal to Christ, the Savior, and one must be loyal to this country which is a Christian republic, as the laws of our country and its jurisprudence are based upon the Scriptures." Other early Pentecostals were more skeptical about patriotism and nationalism. Charles Parham, one of the first Holiness leaders to advocate for tongues, denounced the "Moloch God, Patriotism" and warned that the U.S. was irredeemably corrupt and soon would fall to an evil dictator. (Holiness churches were originally a

branch of Methodism, and many of their leaders were connected to the Keswick conferences in England.) The routine
blending of patriotism and gospel has been one of the chief
ways that evangelicals and Pentecostals—especially whites—
have blurred the theological focus of their movement. Their
nationalistic tendencies became even more pronounced in times
of military conflict and during the Cold War.[8]

Among Pentecostals, the African American–led Church
of God in Christ (COGIC) also saw phenomenal growth between the world wars. COGIC churches had special appeal in
urban centers of the "Great Migration," in which African
Americans relocated in vast numbers from the rural South to
the North and West. Unlike many white Pentecostals, COGIC
leaders emphasized sanctification more than speaking in
tongues. Although preachers such as its founder Charles H.
Mason were COGIC's most recognized leaders, women found
major ministry outlets in COGIC. They served as exemplars of
piety and as evangelists, in spite of COGIC's formal prohibition
on women pastors.[9]

One of the most remarkable early leaders in COGIC was
Sister Rosetta Tharpe, a "guitar evangelist" and the first major
star of gospel music. (Tharpe was posthumously inducted into
the Rock and Roll Hall of Fame in 2017.) Tharpe's mother Ka-
tie Bell Nubin was also a COGIC evangelist. From a young age
Tharpe assisted her mother in revivals from Memphis to Chicago. In Chicago, Tharpe met and married her husband
Thomas, a COGIC minister and evangelist. Rosetta and Thomas partnered in revival work. Evangelists such as Tharpe led the
spectacular expansion of COGIC during the era: Chicago alone
went from having no COGIC congregations in 1915 to twenty-
four in 1928. That was as many churches as the older African
Methodist Episcopal denomination had in Chicago the same

year, but still far behind black Baptists, who had almost a hundred churches in the city. The great gospel singer Mahalia Jackson similarly got her first public opportunities to sing in Chicago's African American Baptist churches, around the same time as Tharpe's early evangelistic work.[10]

COGIC's leaders struggled to balance their commitment to pacifism and a desire to avoid government harassment during World War I. The Bureau of Investigations investigated statements that Bishop Charles Mason and other COGIC pastors had made against military service. Blacks accused of such comments could be in serious peril, especially in the Jim Crow South. COGIC pastor Jesse Payne of Blytheville, Arkansas, was tarred and feathered for allegedly remarking that World War I was a "white man's war." Law enforcement officials feared that Bishop Mason would be lynched for his failure to support the war. Mason recalled that the Holy Ghost was simply prompting him to tell his followers "not to trust in the power of the United States, England, France or Germany, but trust in God."[11] Evangelicals' and Pentecostals' responses to American wars have run the gamut from uncritical patriotism to provocative dissent.

Missions and evangelism remained primary evangelical concerns after the Scopes Trial. For all the attention given to the evolution controversy, missions and church planting were bigger everyday priorities for most evangelical and Pentecostal leaders. Modernists raised difficult questions about missions, however. Growing knowledge of world religions led some critics to ask whether all non-Christians were really bound for hell. Was conversion really necessary, or should missionaries just offer loving service to the non-Christian world? Pearl Buck, the Pulitzer Prize–winning author of *The Good Earth* (1931) and the daughter of missionaries to China, wrote in *Harper's* that

conversionist missions were outdated. Their Christian "forefa-
thers believed sincerely in a magic religion," Buck observed.
"They believed simply and plainly that all who did not hear the
gospel, as they called it, were damned. . . . It goes without question that for most of us this kind of creed has been discarded."[12]

Around the same time, the Laymen's Foreign Missions
Inquiry, funded by liberal Baptist John D. Rockefeller and
headed by Harvard professor William Hocking, produced
similar recommendations. The Inquiry's *Re-thinking Missions*
(1932) expressed a preference for Christian philanthropic work
free from "conscious and direct evangelism." Hocking's report
reconceived traditional proselytism: "Ministry to the secular
needs of men in the spirit of Christ . . . *is* evangelism." The
American Board of Commissioners for Foreign Missions, where
modernist thought had held sway since the 1890s, sent copies
of *Re-thinking Missions* to its missionaries. Traditionalists condemned the report. Clarence Macartney, the conservative pastor of Pittsburgh's First Presbyterian Church, reviled *Re-thinking
Missions* as a "complete repudiation of historic and evangelical
Christianity."[13]

In spite of Buck's assertion that "most of us" had abandoned
the conversionist mandate, the World War II era saw a flowering
of new evangelical missionary and parachurch agencies. These
agencies were a reaction to the fact that many older missionary
groups were influenced by modernism. But some of their im-
petus derived from an older theme: evangelicals' pragmatic
means of sharing the gospel. Burgeoning post-Azusa Pentecostal groups such as COGIC and the Assemblies of God illustrated this ardent flexibility. Evangelicals also founded agencies
such as the Navigators (1933), which started as a mentoring
("discipling") organization in the military but spread to college
campuses and international mission sites. In the 1950s the

Navigators would partner with Billy Graham in "follow up" on professed converts, helping them get established in Christian devotion and Bible study. The Navigators, InterVarsity Christian Fellowship USA (1941), and Campus Crusade for Christ (1951) took advantage of the flourishing college population following World War II to ensure that secular universities had an enduring evangelical witness.

Similarly, Young Life (1941) ministered to high school students and developed a network of evangelistic summer camps. Fellowship of Christian Athletes (FCA) was founded in 1954 by devout mainliners, but by the 1970s it became more aligned with evangelicals, partly via support from Billy Graham. FCA used sports ministry to evangelize athletes and their fans.[14] Finally, international missionary agencies such as World Vision (1950) and Compassion International (1952) served global children in poverty. By the 2010s, Compassion had more than 1 million sponsored children in mission stations around the world. Such organizations illustrate the enduring evangelical penchant for charitable and evangelistic ministry.

World Vision and Compassion were just two of a host of worldwide missionary organizations that evangelicals founded from the 1930s to the 1950s. In the early 1930s J. Gresham Machen created one of the first conservative missionary agencies. The Independent Board for Presbyterian Foreign Missions provided a conservative alternative to the missionary arm of the Presbyterian Church (USA). The formation of the Independent Board led to Machen's suspension from the PCUSA and his founding of the Orthodox Presbyterian Church in 1936. The evangelical linguist William C. Townsend established the Summer Institute of Linguistics (1934) and Wycliffe Bible Translators (1942) to study indigenous languages and produce Bible translations. The National Association of Evangelicals'

Evangelical Foreign Missions Association (EFMA), founded in 1945, fostered cooperation between missionary agencies and the government on logistical issues involved in maintaining stations overseas. The Assemblies of God even purchased surplus B-17 bombers from the government in order to fly missionaries to Latin America. By 1961, the EFMA was working with forty-nine mission boards, representing about five thousand missionaries. By 1992, the EFMA (renamed the Evangelical Fellowship of Mission Agencies) had become the largest global association of missionaries.[15]

Many evangelical denominations continued to sponsor their own mission efforts. Even as the Southern Baptist Convention's Foreign Mission Board struggled to avoid modernist conflicts during the mid-twentieth century, its missionary ranks kept growing. For example, as of March 1950 the Southern Baptist Convention (SBC) had a total of 748 missionaries in twenty-four countries. It had already appointed 41 new missionaries that year, with the bulk of them going to Latin America and Japan (in the wake of the Communist Revolution in China, missionary agencies had to redirect their Asian work). The SBC planned to appoint 50 more missionaries that year. The Plymouth Brethren's Christian Missions in Many Lands supported more than 1,000 missionaries during the same period. These included the most famous American evangelical missionary of the time, Jim Elliot. Along with four other missionaries, Elliot died in an attack by Waorani Indians in Ecuador in 1956. Most missionary work does not receive the media coverage that Jim Elliot's did. *Life* magazine and *Reader's Digest* both gave attention to the episode. But evangelistic missions— including sending missionaries, giving to support them, and praying for them—have been integral to evangelical identity at least since the early 1800s.[16]

Evangelicals dominated American foreign missions by the late twentieth century. The number of missionaries from North America grew from twelve thousand to thirty-five thousand between 1935 and 1980. Mainline missionaries during that period declined from seven thousand to three thousand, while evangelical ones shot up from five thousand to thirty-two thousand. The mainline missionary impulse did not die, but it substantially transitioned into service in nongovernmental agencies such as the Red Cross, or government works such as the Peace Corps. Mainliners largely set aside the conversionist mandate.[17]

By the late 1940s, evangelicals had weathered the fundamentalist-modernist wars. They were engaged in a new round of institution building that would sustain the movement. Yet there remained a sense that evangelicals had lost their way culturally. Although evangelical churches still served as a de facto establishment in much of the South and Midwest, they no longer claimed much public prominence. Gone were the days when traditional Protestants dominated culture-making institutions, from colleges to the media. It was hard to imagine post–World War II evangelicals producing a figure such as Jonathan Edwards, arguably the greatest intellectual in colonial America. J. Gresham Machen was one of the few traditionalist leaders taken seriously in elite media and educational circles. But when Machen died at fifty-five in 1937, he too had become marginal—by choice—to dominant Presbyterian religious and educational life.

After 1945, some evangelicals worked to recover the movement's intellectual respectability. They were laboring against strong headwinds. The countertrends included a secular cultural establishment, a lingering fundamentalist impulse toward insularity, and an evangelical propensity for anti-intellectualism. But from 1945 to the present, there have been halting efforts to reawaken the "evangelical mind." Some of the leaders of this movement, such as Pittsburgh Seminary's John Gerstner, sought to represent evangelical thought within mainline institutions. Others created new evangelical outlets to model the Christian life of the mind.

The key early figure in the renewal of evangelical intel-lectualism was the Northern Baptist Carl F. H. Henry. Henry worked briefly for the *New York Times* as a freelancer prior to attending Wheaton College, arguably the most influential evan-gelical liberal arts college in twentieth-century America. Henry earned a Ph.D. at Boston University, and at Harold John Ock-enga's urging he became one of the first faculty members at Fuller Theological Seminary (founded in 1947). Ockenga be-lieved that evangelicals needed a graduate institution that would not only train pastors but would engage with the broader world of academic study, especially regarding scholarship on the Bible. Fuller Seminary did become an important center for evangelical thought, but it was rocked by disagreements over the doctrine of biblical inerrancy.[18] This debate at Fuller was a throwback to the fundamentalist-modernist controversy. Arguments about the reliability of Scripture hardly ended in the 1920s.

Henry was a perfect choice for the Fuller faculty, given his academic credentials and public voice. He had authored ambitious books titled *Remaking the Modern Mind* (1946) and *The Uneasy Conscience of Modern Fundamentalism* (1947). Ockenga wrote the introduction to *Uneasy Conscience*, which became Henry's best-known work. Henry summoned evan-gelicals out of their fundamentalist ghettoes, exhorting them to enlist against "social evils [such as] aggressive warfare, racial hatred and intolerance, the liquor traffic, and exploitation of labor." An evangelical united front would advance redemptive solutions to social crises, he argued. Evangelicals could do this without succumbing to modernist anti-conversionism or to the fundamentalist tendency to attribute all of humanity's ills to individual sins. "The evangelical task," Henry wrote, "primarily is the preaching of the Gospel, in the interest of individual regeneration by the supernatural grace of God, in such a way that divine redemption can be recognized as the best solution to our problems, individual and social."[19] By the Holy Spirit's power, evangelicals could transform people and societies.

In 1956, Henry became the founding editor of *Christianity Today*, the magazine of record for non-Pentecostal evangelicals. *Christianity Today* was the brainchild of Billy Graham, who said that he hoped the periodical would help give "theological respectability to evangelicals."[20] *Christianity Today* eventually became a general interest magazine rather than one strictly for evangelical academics. In the decades after Henry was its editor, *Christianity Today* vacillated between fundamentalist combativeness (especially during the editorship of Harold Lindsell in the 1970s) and evangelical liberalism (especially in the 2000s and early 2010s). In the meantime, other magazines have challenged *Christianity Today* in certain market segments. These have included *WORLD*, which caters to more theologically and politically conservative readers; *Sojourners*, geared toward political and social liberals; and *Relevant*, pitched to a younger evangelical demographic. These and other publications (and in recent decades websites) remind us that reading evangelical content has been a mark of practicing evangelicals. Being a subscriber to magazines like these is a reliable sign that you are an evangelical.

Evangelicals such as Carl Henry influenced culture through Christian intellectual expression. But for most historic evangelicals (including Henry), cultural influence always *centered* around evangelism. In that gospel work, Billy Graham was one of the two most influential evangelical leaders in American history (the other being George Whitefield). After a conversion experience at age sixteen, Graham graduated from Wheaton College in 1943. He became a Youth for Christ evangelist in 1945. Youth for Christ hosted evangelistic rallies, focusing on returning soldiers and sailors after World War II. Youth for Christ became a formal evangelistic organization in 1946.

Graham was a lot like George Whitefield, except that Whitefield didn't have access to airplanes. Graham traveled relentlessly. During his first year with Youth for Christ, he spoke in forty-seven states. In 1946 he went to the United Kingdom, where he spoke at 360 rallies in six months. Graham visited Oxford University, consciously reflecting upon the Great Awakening legacy of Whitefield and John Wesley. His visit to the UK also introduced Graham to the filling of the Holy Spirit. He met the evangelist Stephen Olford, who had grown up in Angola as the son of Plymouth Brethren missionaries. Graham and Olford spent two days together in Wales, where Olford counseled Graham about his own recent experience of the Spirit's "anointing." Graham agreed that he needed this, and prayed for total dedication to God. In what Graham later described as the turning point of his ministry, he felt that his heart was "flooded" with the Holy Spirit. Graham would never be a full-blown charismatic, but he maintained ties to the Holiness and Pentecostal traditions throughout his career. Recalling similar books written by Hannah Whitall Smith and Dwight Moody, Graham's 1978 *The Holy Spirit: Activating God's Power in Your Life* emphasized the Spirit's felt presence for non-Pentecostal evangelicals.[21]

By 1948 Graham had left Youth for Christ to focus on his own evangelistic campaigns. These culminated in the spectacular 1949 Los Angeles crusade. It lasted for two months and attracted some 350,000 attendees. Through business contacts Graham also drew the attention of newspaper magnate William Randolph Hearst. Though Hearst was not especially pious, he allegedly told his media outlets to "puff Graham." The evangelist likewise attracted the notice of Henry Luce, the child of Presbyterian missionaries and the owner of *Time* and *Life* magazines. Suddenly Graham was catapulted to national fame. Graham was assured of widespread media coverage, which in turn assured big numbers at his crusades. During his career Graham would speak live before more than 200 million people, and he reached hundreds of millions more through writing, radio, and television.[22]

For all his fame, Graham was hardly the only prominent evangelist of the period. For example, Elder Lightfoot Solomon Michaux hosted a phenomenally popular radio program that debuted during the Depression. By 1934, CBS estimated that Michaux had Saturday evening radio audiences of 24 million people. His radio success translated into television, and shortly after the end of World War II Michaux became the first American minister (regardless of ethnicity) to have a television program, and the first African American star in a television series. Some regard Michaux as a founding father of the "prosperity gospel" because he paired traditional Holiness teachings with an emphasis on godly mindset and success. Michaux was staunchly anticommunist, and this stance helped earn him favor with the federal government. FBI officials recruited him in the early 1960s to help undermine the work of Martin Luther King Jr., whom they suspected of communist sympathies. Michaux told his audiences that King's program of legislative reform was not the solution to racial inequality in America. Individual repentance was. Likewise, in the 1940s the Mexican American

Assemblies of God revivalist Robert Fierro pioneered a popular evangelistic Spanish-speaking radio program. Fierro's supporters calculated that some 750,000 people attended his revivals in the U.S., Mexico, and Puerto Rico in the year 1956 alone.[23]

Many other white evangelists prospered during Graham's ascendancy, including Graham's Youth for Christ associate and radio preacher Jack Wyrtzen. Healing evangelists Oral Roberts and Kathryn Kuhlman also enjoyed huge popularity. Roberts got his start as a small-town Pentecostal pastor in Oklahoma but became arguably the most famous televangelist in American history. Although Kuhlman, like Aimee Semple McPherson before her, had endured a divorce and other scandals, her popularity crested from the 1950s to the 1970s, aided by favorable coverage in magazines such as *Redbook* and *Time*. Kuhlman became known for teachings on the Holy Spirit and the spontaneous healings that occurred in her revival services. Although most televangelists were men, Kuhlman had a show on CBS between 1966 and 1976. Her book *I Believe in Miracles* (1962) sold more than 2 million copies in its first three decades.[24]

All these evangelists had enormous followings and platforms. Some of them, such as Roberts and Kuhlman, tended to avoid politics. Other evangelists explicitly commented on political affairs. Michaux was an important figure in the large-scale switch of African Americans from the Republican Party (the party of Lincoln and emancipation) to the Democrats. Michaux made a pathbreaking endorsement of Franklin Roosevelt over Herbert Hoover in 1932. Among all evangelical leaders, however, Billy Graham maintained the most access to elite politicians, including presidents from Dwight Eisenhower to George W. Bush.

No other evangelist has spoken more widely and compellingly about the need to be born again than Graham. Graham also assured audiences that the born-again believer would personally experience God's presence through the Holy Spirit. "When a person is born again," Graham wrote, "the Spirit of God takes the Word of God and makes the child of God. We are born again through the operation of the Holy Spirit."[25] But Graham's influence in Washington, D.C., gave white evangelicals a taste of political power as well. If they could sustain the access that Graham possessed, it could help them save the nation, they thought. They could preserve Christian civilization from atheistic communism and the secular godlessness that seemed to menace America after World War II. The new politicization of evangelicals in this period began not with the culture wars of the 1960s and 1970s, but with their reaction to the Cold War and communism in the decades following World War II. Fundamentalist preachers such as Carl McIntire and Billy James Hargis were blending their gospel with anticommunism by the late 1940s. The threat of international and domestic Bolshevism had become a common feature of Billy Graham's preaching by 1947. Graham called communism "Satan's religion." Evangelicals such as George Whitefield had seen Britain as defending Protestantism against Catholic power in the mid-eighteenth century; many likewise believed that the United States would defend the world from communist godlessness in the twentieth.[26]

Politically engaged evangelicals embraced contradictory priorities, however. They called on the nation to return to a nostalgic past of Christian cultural establishment while exhorting individuals to reject mere cultural Christianity and to be born again. Sometimes it was not clear whether individual conversion or national political influence was their real priority. But these evangelical political insiders were eager to enlist nonevangelical politicians when necessary to regain cultural power. The desire of many white evangelicals to reestablish political influence is at the root of their identity crisis today. That crisis began in the 1950s, became more acute in the 1980s with the advent of the Moral Majority, and went stratospheric with white evangelical voters' overwhelming support for Donald Trump in 2016. By 2016, many critics (some within evangelicalism itself) were wondering whether there was anything substantially spiritual about the movement anymore, or if evangelicals' God-talk just masked earthly ambitions for power.

A major turning point for American evangelicals came in 1951, then, when Billy Graham urged General Dwight Eisenhower to run for president. Graham told Texas oilman Sid Richardson that the American people wanted a "man with honesty, integrity, and spiritual power. I believe the General has it." (Reflecting deep connections between big business and white evangelical leaders, the prodigiously wealthy but nondevout Richardson was one of Graham's major financial backers.) Eisenhower grew up in a pious family and was named for Dwight Moody. Eisenhower had no particular religious commitment as an adult, but he felt that the Judeo-Christian tradition was essential to the health of the American republic. Graham was enthused by Eisenhower's strong anticommunist views, and the presidential candidate invited Graham to help him inject spirituality into his speeches. Graham never formally endorsed Eisenhower, but he dropped plenty of hints about his preferences.[27]

Once Eisenhower won the presidency, he expressed interest in spiritual renewal in America. Graham was ecstatic: "General, you can do more to inspire the American people to a more spiritual way of life than any other man alive!" Soon Eisenhower received baptism into the Presbyterian Church, but he resisted any doctrinal or denominational particularity. Certainly the president did not embrace the need for conversion or other marks of historic evangelicalism. Eisenhower was flippant about theological specificity. "Our government makes no sense unless it is founded on a deeply felt religious faith," Eisenhower said repeatedly, "and I don't care what it is." Eisenhower became one of the great modern architects of American civil religion— the combining of spirituality and patriotism—and he enlisted Graham to help him build it. The alliance of Graham and Eisenhower signaled a crucial trend among white evangelicals, one that would accelerate during the 1980s. Many evangelicals conflated political power and access to Republican leaders with the advancement of God's Kingdom. Relationships with powerful and famous politicians clouded their judgment about who was capable of spiritual leadership. Access to power distracted them from the historic mission of evangelicals. Most evangelicals preferred partners such as Eisenhower, who at least made a generic pretense of piety and expressed respect for Christian social influence. But many white evangelicals suggested that for politicians to "inspire the American people to a more spiritual way of life," born-again faith was no longer required.[28]

5

Two-Track Evangelicals and the New Christian Right

B y 1980, the people I call "Republican insider evangelicals" had become a fixture on the partisan landscape. The formation of Jerry Falwell Sr.'s Moral Majority was an escalation of white evangelicals' quest for influence in Washington, D.C. Falwell was not the most obvious candidate to supplant Billy Graham as the most visible Republican insider evangelical. Although Falwell hosted popular radio and television programs, he was a separatist southern fundamentalist who largely avoided partisan politics until the 1970s. During the civil rights movement Falwell did publicly oppose racial integration. Like many white fundamentalists and evangelicals, Falwell later repudiated segregationism. Paul Weyrich, a Catholic Republican activist and founder of the Heritage Foundation (1973), convinced Falwell in 1979 that there was a "moral majority" (a cousin to Richard Nixon's "silent majority") of Americans who still believed in the Judeo-Christian principles of the Ten Commandments. If someone could rally this cohort it could secure Republican power in the name of traditional morality. Falwell had used the term "moral majority" before, but now it gave a name to his cause. Falwell's Moral Majority and the new Christian Right would indelibly mark white evangelicals' public image for the next four decades.[1]

The Moral Majority concept did not spring from Falwell's and Weyrich's minds alone. It had been simmering for a long time. Evangelical faith always had political implications, as seen in the campaigns for religious liberty, for temperance, and against slavery. By the late 1940s, communism was the leading evangelical political and cultural concern. Soviet and Chinese communism was totalitarian and atheistic; it seemed uniquely antithetical to traditional Christian belief. Anticommunism was widely shared among Republicans and Democrats in the era of the Korean and Vietnam Wars. For evangelicals, fear of communism and nuclear war took on an apocalyptic cast and fueled interest in end-times theology. Billy Graham told an Argentinian audience during the Cuban Missile Crisis (1962) that "the four horses of the apocalypse are preparing for action. The eventual showdown that is now on the horizon is inevitable. We are now on a collision course. . . . The Bible tells us that when world conditions are the worst . . . then will Christ come."[2]

Republicans cultivated evangelical support by presenting themselves as especially tough on communism. As vice president under Eisenhower and as president himself, Richard Nixon made strident anticommunism a defining issue. For GOP insiders, opposition to communism had almost become a species of Christian piety. This spiritualization of anticommunism helped to make the privately profane Nixon, a lapsed Quaker, a favorite of white evangelicals. In 1957, Graham had Nixon speak at his New York City crusade. For many white evangelicals, Nixon was also preferable to John Kennedy in the 1960 presidential election because of enduring Protestant hostility toward Catholics. Graham, the National Association of Evangelicals, and the Southern Baptist Convention all signaled a preference for Nixon over Kennedy, but their support was not enough for Nixon to win (yet).[3]

Many evangelicals perceived communism as just one manifestation of rising threats against Christian civilization. Among the most alarming domestic developments was the Supreme Court's ban on school-sponsored Bible reading and prayer in the early 1960s. These changes seemed to undermine America's ostensible Judeo-Christian establishment, especially in public schools. The decisions on prayer and Bible reading followed symbolic changes in the 1950s that had made a generic Judeo-Christian establishment more conspicuous than at any time before in American history. Congress and the Eisenhower administration added "under God" to the Pledge of Allegiance, put "In God We Trust" on stamps, coins, and bills, and made "In God We Trust" the national motto. (The nation had no official motto before 1956.) The First Amendment prohibited Congress from creating an established religion, but into the 1950s many still understood this merely as precluding an official national denomination. The national acknowledgments of God garnered widespread support, not only among evangelicals but among Catholics, Jews, and mainline Protestants. The fact that "under God" and "In God We Trust" expressed a vague "ceremonial deism" hardly detracted from their value for supporters. An attempted May 1954 constitutional amendment affirming the national authority of Jesus Christ did not pass in Congress. The bipartisan anticommunist coalition behind "In God We Trust" could not coalesce around adding explicitly Christian rhetoric to the formal documents of the nation.[4]

When the Supreme Court scaled back the nation's Judeo-Christian establishment in the early 1960s, many evangelicals became frustrated. In *Engel v. Vitale* (1962), the Supreme Court ruled that New York had violated the First Amendment by adopting the "Regents' Prayer," a generic prayer of dependence upon "Almighty God" at the beginning of each school day. The liberal Baptist Hugo Black argued that state-sponsored prayer represented an establishment of religion. Evangelical reaction to *Engel v. Vitale* was mixed. The National Association of Evangelicals said the decision was "regrettable." Billy Graham was concerned that the watching world might wonder whether America really was a "nation under God." Anecdotal evidence suggests that a number of African American Baptist pastors opposed the decision, although Martin Luther King Jr. thought the reasoning in *Engel* was sound. *Christianity Today* accepted the decision, too, arguing that the Regents' Prayer was so vague that it was not worth defending. Graham eventually agreed, acknowledging that true believers should not want the government to compose prayers for them.[5]

Some found the decision in *Abington School District v. Schempp* (1963) more alarming than *Engel*. In *Abington School District*, the Supreme Court struck down a Pennsylvania law mandating daily Bible readings in schools. The King James Bible—still the preferred translation of many Protestants—had been a staple of American education since the colonial era. As of 1963, only eleven states had banned Bible readings in schools, while twelve states mandated Bible readings. The rest permitted Bible readings, but they were not mandatory. Bible reading in schools was one of the clearest examples of a Protestant cultural establishment. So when the court declared that mandatory Bible readings were unconstitutional, it struck many observers as outrageous and possibly communist-inspired. The Southern

Baptist senator and segregationist stalwart Strom Thurmond of South Carolina told *CBS News* that *Abington School District* "drives another nail in the coffin being prepared for a free and God-fearing America by the secularists and Socialists of the world." Harold John Ockenga said that a turn toward secularism in the schools would leave the nation "in the same position as Communist Russia."[6]

The National Association of Evangelicals, along with many Catholics and fundamentalists, called for a constitutional amendment to counteract *Engel* and *Abington School District*. In spite of Thurmond's fulminations, Southern Baptists were divided on the issue. The SBC passed a resolution in 1964 opposing an amendment that would overturn the decisions. Many Southern Baptists were friendlier to church-state separation than were other evangelicals. Reflecting their enduring anti-Catholic sentiment, some Baptists worried that weakening the establishment clause would open the door for government support for Catholic schools. To some evangelicals, support for Catholic education was an even less desirable outcome than banning formal prayer and Bible reading from public schools.[7]

Not all evangelicals militantly supported school prayer and Bible reading, but *Engel* and *Abington School District* still influenced the emerging union between white evangelicals and the Republican Party. Many evangelicals saw these decisions as attacking what was left of Christianity's established cultural position. Concerned Christians started looking for politicians who would stop further attacks. Republicans recognized Christians' cultural anxiety as an opportunity to win voters, especially in the traditionally Democratic white South. In 1964, the Republican Party endorsed a school prayer amendment. Such an amendment has been introduced many times since in Congress, sometimes with bipartisan support. But it has never passed with the requisite two-thirds majorities in the House and Senate. For example, a Senate school prayer amendment got only fifty-six votes in 1984, even though polls showed that some 80 percent of Americans supported it.[8]

Such amendments have typically stipulated that they wished to protect only voluntary prayer in schools. In 2016, the GOP platform still affirmed the "rights of religious students to engage in voluntary prayer at public school events."[9] Republicans have not done much to bring about substantive legal change on school prayer. Indicating formal support for it has been of great value to the GOP, however, in cultivating its white evangelical base.

In the early 1960s, many American Christians were more concerned about civil rights than the Supreme Court's decisions on school prayer and Bible reading. Some of the most visible leaders of the civil rights movement, such as Ella Baker, Martin Luther King Jr., and the Unitarian Howard Thurman, were not recognizably evangelical, even if they were formed by the black church. (King's preaching drew on evangelical themes, but his theology often reflected the modernism of his doctoral education at Boston University.) Many of the "local people" in the campaigns for civil rights did embrace evangelical beliefs. One was Fannie Lou Hamer, who worked to register black voters in Mississippi. In 1963, she endured torture from police and prisoners at a Winona, Mississippi, jail in retaliation for her activism. Driven by her deep faith, Hamer would not give up the fight for civil rights. Charles Marsh, whose book *God's Long Summer* poignantly documented the roles that faith played in the struggle for and against civil rights, wrote that Hamer was inspired by a piety "evangelical in the most vigorous sense of the term, a robust and disciplined love of Jesus of Nazareth, of the whole scandalous story of his life, death, and resurrection."[10] Hamer, the daughter of sharecroppers, would expose the white-dominated Democratic Party's passivity on civil rights in televised testimony at the 1964 Democratic National Convention.

John Perkins was one of the African American civil rights leaders most closely aligned with evangelicals. Many in Perkins's family were bootleggers, and he was the first person in his family to accept Christ as Savior. Perkins had formerly seen religion as a distraction for oppressed southern blacks, but after moving from Mississippi to California he began to study the Bible for himself and realized that he needed salvation. When he came to the moment of conversion, he exclaimed, "God for a black man? Yes, God for a black man! *This* black man! Me! That morning I said yes to Jesus Christ."[11] Perkins returned to Mississippi in 1960, establishing a church and evangelistic ministry. Over time, Perkins expanded his focus from pure evangelism to social and civil rights advocacy. After helping to organize a civil rights boycott in Mendenhall, Mississippi, Perkins was arrested and viciously beaten by highway patrol officers and a sheriff ironically named Jonathan Edwards.

In the following decades, Perkins would become a pioneer of holistic community ministry. He is arguably the most important figure in introducing African Americans' social justice concerns to white evangelicals. He became a popular speaker at majority-white evangelical colleges and served on the board of evangelical organizations such as Prison Fellowship, World Vision, and the National Association of Evangelicals. Perkins is uniquely positioned because of his combination of experience in civil rights and his unquestioned evangelical beliefs. Perkins's evangelistic and social ministry is one of the clearest fulfillments of what Carl Henry had called for in *The Uneasy Conscience of Modern Fundamentalism.*[12]

White evangelical responses to civil rights ranged from cautious support to staunch opposition. Some white evangelicals expressed sympathy but worried about radical influences in the civil rights movement. Many remained silent, or reminded fellow whites about the spiritual nature of the church and the necessity of sticking to the gospel. (This principle did not seem to apply when white Christians were advocating for prohibition, anticommunism, or prayer in schools.) Overall, most white evangelicals did nothing to assist the civil rights movement. Blacks who held evangelical beliefs realized that many of their white compatriots did not care to do much about segregation, inequality, and racial violence. This was not a surprise, given white passivity during Reconstruction and the era of mass lynchings. Frustration over white inaction helped push African American Christians further away from the formal evangelical movement. Their disappointment also prompted the formation of the National Black Evangelical Association in 1963.[13]

Billy Graham initially allowed segregated seating at crusades in southern cities, but he quietly ended the practice starting in 1953 in Chattanooga. (His revivalist predecessors Dwight Moody and Billy Sunday had both allowed segregation at their meetings.) We should not mistake Graham for a civil rights activist, but he did stake his considerable reputation on desegregation. He also appeared with Martin Luther King Jr. at a New York City revival in 1957. King offered a prayer at the assembly. Mahalia Jackson also performed there, beginning a tradition of African American vocalists singing at Graham crusades. Graham's moderate pro–civil rights stance earned him the ire of many fundamentalists, and hate mail from the Ku Klux Klan. But in 1958, the segregationist governor of Texas introduced Graham at a crusade in San Antonio over the protests of local Baptist ministers. King himself warned Graham about the risk of implicitly endorsing segregation. Graham and King would continue to interact occasionally, but they were not close friends. Graham felt more drawn to black ministers such as the evangelical E. V. Hill, a Missionary Baptist pastor in Los Angeles who served in the Billy Graham Evangelistic Association. Hill had helped to found King's Southern Christian Leadership Conference, and he remained active in addressing the needs of the poor in Los Angeles. But Hill became a conspicuous supporter of Republicans, offering a prayer at Richard Nixon's second inauguration.[14]

Carl Henry and *Christianity Today* associate editor Frank Gaebelein wanted to enlist directly in the civil rights movement. In 1965, Henry assigned Gaebelein to cover the protest march in Selma, Alabama. Gaebelein was so moved by what he saw that he left the journalists' section and joined the marchers. But J. Howard Pew, an oil magnate and supporter of *Christianity Today*, and Nelson Bell, Graham's father-in-law and an editorial advisor at the magazine, were uncomfortable with civil rights activism. They suppressed Gaebelein's coverage of the march. Some major black clergymen, such as the National Baptist Convention's J. H. Jackson, opposed King's tactics of direct resistance, too, so it is unsurprising that most white Christian leaders did not rally around his protests.[15]

Conversely, few white evangelicals supported the civil rights movement as zealously as John Alexander, a philosophy teacher at Wheaton College. Alexander's journal *Freedom Now* addressed racial issues in terms that appealed to an evangelical audience. John Perkins was one of the earliest contributors to *Freedom Now*. Alexander and the Anabaptist-influenced evangelical Ron Sider, author of the influential *Rich Christians in an Age of Hunger* (1977), became part of a small but vocal white evangelical Left that emerged by the 1960s. Left-leaning evangelicals insisted that sin was built into social structures, not just individual actions. Sider said that the traditional evangelical focus on individual sin meant that many privileged believers failed to see the "sins of institutional racism, unjust economic structures and militaristic institutions which destroy people just as much as do alcohol and drugs."[16]

Fundamentalists such as Bob Jones Sr. and Jerry Falwell Sr. openly opposed desegregation. White evangelicals tended to be exceedingly cautious about civil rights reform, if not actively opposed. The South also produced outspoken evangelical segregationists, including W. A. Criswell, pastor of First Baptist Church, Dallas, where Graham kept his church membership for many years. (Graham was not a regular attendee because of his travel schedule.) When the Southern Baptist Convention endorsed the Supreme Court's desegregation ruling in *Brown v. Board of Education* (1954), Criswell was indignant. Criswell defended segregation before the South Carolina legislature in 1956, though he based his argument mostly upon cultural norms rather than biblical exegesis. Criswell publicly abandoned his segregationist views once he became SBC president in 1968. A number of Deep South Baptists, especially in Mississippi, were angry with the SBC's Christian Life Commission (predecessor to the Ethics and Religious Liberty Commission) for its relatively progressive stances on race issues. Some segregationist SBC churches and pastors threatened to (or actually did) stop giving to the SBC's Cooperative Program because of the Christian Life Commission's views. Few surpassed the publicly virulent racism of the Free Will Baptist evangelist James "Catfish" Cole, however, whose tent meetings in 1950s North Carolina doubled as evangelistic events for Jesus and the Ku Klux Klan.[17]

Typical of many white evangelical leaders, Graham's work ran along two main tracks: politics and evangelism. As Graham declared at the Lausanne Congress on World Evangelization in Switzerland in 1974, "When I go to preach the Gospel, I go as an ambassador for the Kingdom of God—not America." Making the distinction between partisanship and gospel was not easy in practice. Nevertheless, Graham's ministry in the 1960s increasingly turned toward the world. His global ministry heightened his sensitivity to race issues in America. He spent significant time in centers of evangelical faith in the Global South. In 1960, he toured sixteen cities in ten African countries, insisting on integrated audiences wherever he went. He declined to visit South Africa because the apartheid system there would not allow for an integrated crusade. Graham preached before a total of 570,000 people on the Africa tour, with 35,000 responding to Graham's gospel invitations. In the American media, the details of Graham's evangelistic overtures generated little enduring interest, especially after the Los Angeles crusade. Although Graham softened his hellfire preaching during his career, his basic message of salvation though Christ remained constant. That gospel did not make news. But politics did.[18]

Graham was the most visible evangelist of the era, but he was hardly the only national figure proclaiming the gospel. Another was Tom Skinner, who grew up in the post–World War II era as the son of a black Baptist preacher in Harlem, but as a rebellious young man became a leader of a New York street gang. At fifteen, Skinner experienced radical conversion through listening to an evangelistic radio program. He told fellow gang members that he had accepted Christ and was leaving the gang. Stories of conversion out of gang life resonated among many evangelicals. For example, the Puerto Rican Pentecostal evangelist Nicky Cruz was converted out of a gang under the ministry of the charismatic evangelist David Wilkerson. Wilkerson and Cruz's encounter was depicted in the best-selling book *The Cross and the Switchblade* (1962), which also became a 1970 movie starring Pat Boone and Erik Estrada.[19]

Skinner, for his part, met Martin Luther King Jr. in 1958 and participated in the Freedom Rides into the segregated South. Skinner made a major mark as an evangelist, holding a remarkable crusade at Harlem's Apollo Theater in 1962, with ten thousand people in attendance and twenty-two hundred responding to his gospel invitation. Skinner came to the attention of Graham's old Youth for Christ colleague Jack Wyrtzen, who invited him to join the speaking rotation at Wyrtzen's crusades. Skinner held major assemblies across North America and the Caribbean. He became widely known through the Moody Bible Institute radio network, speaking engagements at schools such as Wheaton College, and positive coverage in *Christianity Today*.

But trouble began as Skinner started focusing on social injustices as much as personal conversion. He gave a controversial address at InterVarsity's 1970 Urbana missions conference in Illinois, a key event for college students interested in international missions. Skinner lambasted the white evangelical church for its complicity in slavery, Jim Crow laws, and segregation. The next year, Moody radio canceled Skinner's program because he was becoming too "political." This was another instance of white and black evangelicals clashing over racial topics and the boundaries of "political" preaching. Both sides engaged with political issues, but Skinner's focus on race relations and social justice elicited white unease and cancellations. Skinner grew distant from white evangelicals, focusing more on black leadership, inner-city youth, sports ministry as chaplain of the Washington Redskins, and working with the Congressional Black Caucus.[20]

The evangelistic impulse kept seeding white-led ministries with influential people of color, however. Billy Graham recruited

a remarkable group of evangelists, translators, and other col-
laborators from around the world to assist in his crusades. One
of his most significant protégés was the Argentinian-born evangelist Luis Palau. Palau converted when he was seventeen, through
hearing Graham's *Hour of Decision* radio program in Argentina.
Palau met Graham in 1962 and began working for him as a Spanish translator. With Graham's assistance, Palau launched his own
evangelistic ministry in 1970. Palau said that he "copied everything" that Graham did. Palau made major inroads in Central
and South America, befriending leading politicians and securing
as much media access as possible. Palau was not a Pentecostal,
however, which limited his appeal among many Latin American
Protestants. Starting in the late 1990s, Palau began hosting city-
wide festivals throughout the Americas and Europe. As of the
mid-2000s, his ministry estimated that Palau had spoken before
some 21 million people in seventy countries.[21]

Another member of Graham's global cohort was Bilquis
Sheikh, a Pakistani noblewoman who accepted Christ after
receiving intense visions and dreams about Jesus. Sheikh was
encouraged to pursue these experiences by Pentecostal missionaries, and soon she received Holy Spirit baptism. Then she
saw a vision of Jesus's face. "Something surged through me," she
wrote, "wave after wave of purifying ocean breakers, flooding
me to the tips of my fingers and toes, washing my soul." Sheikh
spoke at a Graham conference on missions in Singapore in 1968.
Her conversion narrative, *I Dared to Call Him Father* (1978),
has been translated into many languages and has become one
of the most popular evangelical testimonies by a former Muslim.
Her autobiography remains a steady seller in the U.S. today.
Although missionaries have converted relatively few Muslims
to Christianity, the topic of Muslim evangelization is of perennial interest to American evangelicals. That interest surged in

the years following the September 11, 2001, terrorist attacks. The Muslim conversion genre produced other successful autobiographies such as Mosab Hassan Yousef's *Son of Hamas* (2010) and the late Nabeel Qureshi's *Seeking Allah, Finding Jesus* (2014).[22]

Graham's 1968 Singapore meeting was one of a series that his association convened in the spirit of the 1910 Edinburgh World Missionary Conference. The most significant evangelical missions conference of the era was the 1974 Lausanne, Switzerland, assembly. Graham and other Anglo-Americans dominated the Lausanne Congress, but figures from the "majority world" and Global South churches took a prominent role, too. Eleven of the thirty-one members of the Lausanne planning committee were from Latin America, Africa, or Asia. (All committee members were male. In recent decades, white evangelical leaders have been quicker to address the marginalization of nonwhite men than that of women in such settings.) The congress crafted the Lausanne Covenant, a landmark statement about missions. It affirmed the need for individual conversion of all people and the primacy of the Holy Spirit in missions. "We believe in the power of the Holy Spirit," signatories affirmed. "The Father sent his Spirit to bear witness to his Son; without his witness ours is futile. Conviction of sin, faith in Christ, new birth and Christian growth are all his work. Further, the Holy Spirit is a missionary spirit; thus evangelism should arise spontaneously from a Spirit-filled church."[23]

Lausanne delegates split over the extent to which missionaries should address social justice and collective sins. Anglo-American representatives expressed skepticism, but South Americans such as the Baptists Samuel Escobar and René Padilla insisted that a gospel focused only on individual repentance was not the whole gospel. In his autobiography, Carl Henry explained that Lausanne "postponed rather than resolved the conflicts and ambiguities in contemporary evangelicalism over the Church's socio-political involvement." That tension also manifests itself in the split today between many African American and Hispanic leaders who want the church to address racial justice, and white evangelicals who are wary of the "social gospel" as a distraction from the church's core business.[24]

During the twentieth century, the center of world Christianity shifted to the Global South. When we envision the "typical" world Christian today, historian Philip Jenkins says, we should imagine "a woman living in a village in Nigeria, or in a Brazilian *favela*." The years after 1965 saw an increasing awareness of the global church among American evangelical leaders such as Graham. Those decades also saw a transformation of American evangelicals into a more fully multiethnic movement. American evangelicalism is becoming less characterized by the traditional white/African American binary. Revisions to American immigration law in 1965 changed who was coming into America. Hispanic immigrants remain the dominant group. In 2010, more than 50 million Hispanics lived in the U.S., an increase of 15 million since 2000. Sixty-three percent of the 50 million Hispanics were of Mexican heritage, and many of them were recent immigrants to the U.S. The majority of Mexican Americans and others of Latin American heritage have a Catholic background, but growing numbers of them are evangelicals and Pentecostals.[25]

Fourteen million other people living in America in 2010 were of Asian background. The census counted about 3.3 million Chinese Americans and 1.4 million Korean Americans. There are significant numbers of evangelicals among both groups. Koreans and Korean Americans have played an especially prominent role in the American evangelical world since 1965. Since the 1960s, South Korea's Protestant population—which is mostly evangelical—has grown at a phenomenal rate, and its churches and evangelical agencies developed a reputation for ambitious missionary work, including in the U.S. One of the most dynamic missions-sending Korean organizations is University Bible Fellowship (UBF), founded in 1961 by Southern Presbyterian missionary Sarah Barry and Korean Presbyterian pastor Samuel (Chang-Woo) Lee. This nondenominational evangelical association turned into a global powerhouse, with more than fourteen hundred Korean missionaries serving in about three hundred UBF chapters in eighty-eight countries by the year 2008. More than a third of those chapters were in North America. Other key Asian American evangelical leaders in recent years include Taiwanese American Tom Lin, who became the president of InterVarsity USA in 2016, and Chinese American Francis Chan, a former megachurch pastor in Simi Valley, California, and author of books such as the best-selling *Crazy Love* (2008).[26]

Immigrants to the U.S. since 1965 have been disproportionately Christian, although immigration has also increased the number of Muslims, Hindus, and adherents of other faiths in America. Numerically, however, the most powerful religious trend caused by post-1965 immigration has been to make American Christianity—including evangelicalism—more ethnically diverse. This begins with the overwhelmingly Christian background of Mexican Americans. The same can be said for the religious heritage of most other Latin American and Caribbean immigrants. Christians are overrepresented among Korean, Vietnamese, Arab, and other immigrants, too, when compared to the percentage of Christians in their home countries. Growing numbers are coming to the U.S. from sub-Saharan

Africa, and many of those Africans are evangelicals or Pentecostals. Research through the 2000s suggested that about two-thirds of the post-1965 immigrants were Christians. The numerical impact of these Christian immigrants is probably greatest among U.S. Catholics, but they have also transformed American evangelical and Pentecostal churches. On a daily basis, the ministries of immigrant-led churches are perhaps more representative of evangelicals than the political labors of the Republican evangelical insiders, in spite of the disproportionate news coverage given to the latter.[27]

As we ask, "Who is an evangelical?" we should give granular attention to a few of these immigrant-influenced churches and evangelical groups. Demographically, they represent the evangelical future. As of the 2010s, there were about a million Latino Protestants living in Los Angeles County, and three-quarters of those were evangelicals or Pentecostals. About 50 percent of Assemblies of God members in Southern California are Latinos.[28]

Los Angeles–based Victory Outreach/Alcance Victoria, founded in 1967, represents the kind of dynamic ministry that fuels Hispanic Pentecostalism in America. Victory Outreach's founder, the Puerto Rican New Yorker Sonny Arguinzoni, experienced conversion under the ministry of Nicky Cruz, the subject of David Wilkerson's *The Cross and the Switchblade*. Once converted, Arguinzoni stopped using drugs and vowed to become a minister like Cruz. He enrolled at La Puente Bible College in the Los Angeles area, an Assemblies of God institution and one of the oldest Hispanic-focused colleges in the nation. At La Puente, Arguinzoni met and married his wife Julie, also a devout Pentecostal. Sonny Arguinzoni began working among gang members and drug users in Los Angeles in the 1960s. The Arguinzonis' evangelistic work, drug rehabilitation, and rescue sheltering flourished into Victory Outreach. The ministry became an association of churches and rehab centers. Currently Victory Outreach claims over seven hundred churches and ministries in thirty-three countries. Its website claims you can find a Victory Outreach congregation everywhere from "London to Los Angeles, Manila to Mexicali." Churches such as Victory Outreach have changed the nature of American evangelicalism as much or more than churches that are better known among whites, such as Rick Warren's Los Angeles–area Saddleback Church. Founded in 1980 in Orange County, Saddleback had developed into one of America's largest churches by the 1990s. Warren's *The Purpose Driven Life* (2002) also became one of the best-selling books of the 2000s, with tens of millions of copies sold.[29]

Boston, like Los Angeles, is one of the epicenters of a "quiet revival" of immigrant church planting since 1965. Signs of decline marked many of Boston's white-led churches during those decades. But even before 1965, Boston had begun to see new life among immigrant churches. The Chinese Evangelical Church, which would become the area's largest Chinese Christian congregation, opened in 1961 under the pastorate of James Tan. Park Street Church (where Harold John Ockenga was pastor until 1969) helped Tan's church gain legal incorporation, even as Park Street and similar churches developed their own targeted ministries to Boston-area international students. South Boston also saw the emergence of several new Pentecostal churches ministering primarily to Puerto Ricans in the 1960s. Latino-focused churches proliferated across the metropolitan Boston area, and by 2000 there were at least eighty-five Spanish-language Protestant churches in the city. Boston's quiet revival also touched certain mainline churches, which over time became heavily Latino or populated by other immigrant groups. The

León de Judá Church, affiliated with American Baptists, began meeting in 1982 and became one of the largest Hispanic-led congregations in New England. Media reports often cover the swelling number of churches—especially mainline Protestant congregations—closing in America. Less often reported is the fact that conservative, Pentecostal, or new immigrant churches have routinely purchased church buildings from declining or closing congregations.[30]

Haitians also established a major Protestant presence in Boston, in spite of the strong French Catholic tradition in Haiti. In 1969, the First Haitian Baptist Church became the first Protestant congregation catering to Haitians in the city. By 2000, there were more than fifty Haitian Protestant congregations in the Boston area. Other immigrant congregations, including Brazilian, Korean, and Nigerian ones, have appeared. Not that African American or white church growth has been absent in New England. The Southern Baptist Convention has made a significant effort to open new churches in the Northeast in recent years. The African American–led Jubilee Christian Church (affiliated with the Church of God, Anderson, Indiana, a Holiness denomination) grew to about seven thousand members by the mid-2000s, making it one of the largest churches in the Northeast. All this growth has dramatically increased the (recorded) number of churches in the metropolitan Boston area, from about three hundred to six hundred between the late 1960s and 2000.[31]

Moreover, congregations led by people of color and immigrants are often underreported in standard religious surveys. Such congregations are often independent or part of associations with which religious statisticians are not familiar. They commonly meet in storefronts, or they share church space with established congregations. The number of these new evangelical and Pentecostal congregations across the U.S., then, may be significantly larger than conventional survey data would suggest. In any case, as illustrated by Boston's church growth, these kinds of churches are transforming the profile of American Christianity, including evangelicalism and Pentecostalism.[32]

On the whole, Protestant immigrant churches—especially those led by Latinos and Africans—are friendly to charismatic and Pentecostal worship styles. The Charismatic Renewal movement of the 1960s and 1970s impacted a number of white-led mainline, evangelical, and Catholic congregations, too. While "Pentecostal" generally refers to those affiliated with the historical denominations such as the Church of God in Christ or the Assemblies of God, "charismatic" is a more general term for those who focus on the Spirit and engage in expressive worship. Charismatic believers and congregations appear, at least in small numbers, in almost every Christian denomination.

Charismatic practices especially took hold among evangelical churches connected to the counterculture of the 1960s. The Jesus youth movement was centered in San Francisco and Los Angeles. The most influential organizational manifestation of the Jesus movement was in the Calvary Chapel association of churches, led by Pastor Chuck Smith. Smith had grown up in Aimee Semple McPherson's denomination, the International Church of the Foursquare Gospel, but founded Calvary Chapel in Costa Mesa, California, in 1965. It originally ministered to middle-class whites, but Smith and his wife Kay developed a concern for the burgeoning youth community at neighboring Huntington Beach. This resulted in a massive influx of hippie converts into Calvary Chapel, which also established a communal house called the House of Miracles, following the example of the youth ministry of David Wilkerson.[33]

One of the most influential Calvary Chapel leaders was Lonnie Frisbee, a long-haired Jesus look-alike who emphasized the baptism of the Holy Spirit and speaking in tongues. Frisbee also highlighted what new charismatics would call "power evangelism," or proselytism driven by demonstrations of the Spirit's might, such as physical healings. Frisbee and Chuck Smith were not in complete accord on charismatic gifts, as Smith tended to worry more than Frisbee about Pentecostal excesses. This tension eventually led Frisbee and former rock musician John Wimber to found the Vineyard Churches in 1982, with Chuck Smith's permission. The Vineyard Churches began with Wimber's eighteen-hundred-member Calvary Chapel of Yorba Linda. Frisbee would become marginalized due to a divorce and ongoing struggles with homosexuality, which most self-identifying evangelicals saw as contradicting the biblical design for sex and marriage. But the fast-growing Vineyard Churches now have more than twenty-four hundred churches in ninety-five countries. One of the most famous Vineyard congregations is the Toronto Airport Christian Fellowship, the site of the controversial 1990s revival called the Toronto Blessing. This revival attracted much media attention as well as scorn from "cessationist" evangelicals. It included ecstatic experiences such as "holy laughter," or loud and seemingly uncontrollable laughing as attendees expressed joy in the Spirit. People from all over the world, including many American charismatics, made their way to Toronto to experience the revival.[34]

As these demographic and spiritual changes were sweeping evangelicalism after 1965, certain white evangelicals were aligning themselves more closely with the Republican Party. These Republican insider evangelicals brought many of their followers with them. President Nixon courted evangelicals and managed to get all but the hardest-edged fundamentalist leaders to support him, instead of segregationist George Wallace, in the 1968 election. Nixon had little interest in Christian devotion. But he projected a pious image in public, including holding Sunday church services at the White House. Billy Graham spoke at the first Nixon White House service, and coordinated the list of service speakers with the administration. Nixon showed meager understanding of what evangelicals believed, but they were valued members of his "silent majority." "The Billy Grahams and all the rest, the Southern Baptists and so forth, they've got character," Nixon once said in a White House conversation. White House officials huddled regularly with Graham during the 1972 campaign. Although Graham declined to give the administration his mailing list, he publicly announced during the fall 1972 campaign that he would vote for Nixon over George McGovern. Harold John Ockenga did, too. This white evangelical alliance with Nixon did generate some resistance to Graham, including among missions-minded young evangelicals. In 1970, for the first time, Graham was not invited to speak at InterVarsity's Urbana missions conference, the same conference where Tom Skinner had given his controversial address on race.[35]

By 1972, Graham had effectively become a Republican consultant. He still worked on the traditional track of evangelism, of course, as seen in the Lausanne Congress of 1974 and his global crusades. His ministry in the U.S. was increasingly limited to white middle-class people, though. A summer 1972 Graham crusade in Cleveland, by then a majority-black city, drew an audience that was 99 percent white. When the Watergate scandal threatened Nixon's presidency, Graham initially defended him. But eventually Graham realized that Nixon's virtuous pretensions had been a sham. For a time, the embarrassed Graham took a step back from partisan politics.[36]

The collapse of Nixon's presidency still left politically oriented evangelicals some prominent issues on which to focus. One was the defeat of the Equal Rights Amendment (originally proposed in 1971), which sought to guarantee women equality under the law. Many evangelicals saw it as an attack on traditional family and gender norms. Another priority was the pro-life cause, although it took time for some evangelicals to join that movement. Some, such as Carl Henry, did speak out as states began to liberalize their abortion laws in the late 1960s, but many evangelicals regarded the issue as a secondary one. The Southern Baptist Convention in 1971 even passed a resolution promoting the *legality* of abortion when necessary to protect the "emotional, mental, and physical health of the mother." First Baptist Dallas pastor W. A. Criswell argued that abortion should be permitted, if necessary, up to the moment of birth. The SBC equivocated about abortion for years following the Supreme Court's *Roe v. Wade* decision in 1973, although the NAE and *Christianity Today* registered immediate concern about *Roe*. African American Protestants were more likely than whites—even white Catholics—to oppose abortion in the early 1970s. Civil rights activist Fannie Lou Hamer, for example, said that "legal abortion is legal murder." But during the 1976 election, Democrats started to abandon their traditional opposition to abortion. As it had done with school prayer, the GOP seized on the opportunity to endorse a right-to-life amendment. This was initially designed to appeal to Catholics more than evangelicals, since devout Catholics were more uniformly pro-life than evangelicals were.[37]

The 1976 election saw a scramble for the allegiance of white evangelical voters. Democrats were still in the game. They nominated the Georgia Baptist Jimmy Carter, one of the most overtly pious Christians ever to run for president. Carter was comfortable talking about his own born-again experience. But he supported abortion rights and the Equal Rights Amendment (ERA). Carter also gave an interview to *Playboy* magazine during the campaign that many saw as inappropriate. Not only was the soft-core pornographic outlet unseemly for a self-professed evangelical, but Carter spoke awkwardly about how lust was born in one's heart and how he had "committed adultery in my heart many times." The *Playboy* interview prompted Jerry Falwell Sr. to start criticizing Carter on his radio show. Republican president Gerald Ford was an Episcopalian who also affirmed (without much conviction) that he was born again. Ford courted conservative Protestants by visiting Criswell's First Baptist Dallas and becoming the first sitting president to address the Southern Baptist Convention annual meeting. Ford, however, was damaged by his association with Richard Nixon, and his White House was full of supporters (including his wife Betty) of the ERA and abortion rights.[38]

It was Ronald Reagan who truly began to charm rank-and-file white evangelical voters for the GOP. Reagan was not especially devout, and he was divorced. He had signed a law liberalizing access to abortion as well as the nation's first no-fault divorce law, as governor of California. But Reagan had made a personal Christian commitment in 1966, becoming affiliated with the evangelical-leaning Bel Air Presbyterian Church in Hollywood. He cultivated contacts with evangelical and Pentecostal leaders, including Graham and the singer/actor Pat Boone, a devout charismatic. Reagan, as the "Great Communicator" and a former actor, knew exactly how to talk to evangelicals. He was even known to share his faith personally in terms that evangelicals would readily recognize. Though Reagan would not be able to displace Ford in 1976, his GOP primary challenge that year heralded a white evangelical tsunami that would deluge Carter in 1980.[39]

In 1976, the news media and polling agencies realized that the "born-again" vote was a seminal political factor. The Gallup organization in 1976 began asking people whether they had been "born again." The emergence of *evangelical* as a common term in news coverage of politics was a major landmark in the development of the contemporary evangelical crisis. Prompted by Carter's campaign, *Newsweek* also declared 1976 to be the "year of the evangelical." The media's frequent use of "born again" and "evangelical" formally connected those terms to political behavior. Polling data on evangelicals and politics was easily packaged for publication. From 1976 forward, "evangelical" would increasingly connote the white religious Republican base. Evangelical leaders enjoyed the increased media attention, but they failed to recognize that they were losing control of the public's perception of their movement.[40]

As the 1980 election approached, white evangelical opposition to abortion grew staunch. Although the Bible did not address abortion directly, it did make clear that God created the unborn child. In Psalm 139, the psalmist praised God because he had "knitted me together in my mother's womb" (English Standard Version). For critics of the procedure, abortion had a clear victim: the unborn child. To most white evangelicals, abortion also did not seem as ethically complex as issues such as poverty or racial inequality.

Evangelicals still needed pro-life advocates to help them see this was not just a Catholic issue. The key voice in cementing evangelical opposition to abortion was the eccentric apologetics writer Francis Schaeffer. In 1979, Schaeffer and the pediatrician C. Everett Koop (a future surgeon general under Reagan) pro-

duced the pro-life film *Whatever Happened to the Human Race?*
This film convinced many evangelicals that abortion was the
greatest moral crisis of the day. Wearing his trademark white
goatee, Schaeffer explained that the abortion industry was the
product of secular humanist thought and its contempt for biblical morality. Jerry Falwell Sr. was one of many convinced by
Schaeffer to make abortion a top partisan priority. Schaeffer's
works also influenced leaders of the "conservative resurgence"
in the Southern Baptist Convention. The resurgence began in
1979 and turned the SBC in a uniformly conservative direction.
In 1980, the SBC finally passed a resolution recommending an
antiabortion constitutional amendment, breaking with the
Georgia Baptist in the White House.[41]

Exactly what issue was the most important in the Moral
Majority's birth is unclear. Falwell and his followers attributed
the rise of the movement to a cluster of culture war controversies: school prayer, the ERA, homosexual rights, gambling,
pornography, abortion, and other concerns. They also wanted
to protect Christian schools from the Internal Revenue Service.
The IRS had already stripped fundamentalist Bob Jones University of its tax-exempt status in 1976 because of the school's
prohibition on interracial dating. In 1978, the IRS declared that
private schools must meet minimal minority enrollment standards or lose their tax-exempt privileges. Many private Christian
schools, including Falwell's own Lynchburg Christian Academy
in Virginia (1967), had been founded in the wake of public
school integration. Although it had no written policy against
integration, Falwell's school did not admit any nonwhite students
for two years. The Lynchburg newspaper described it as a "private school for white students" at its opening. Critics charged
that such "segregation academies" subverted integration, even
as they spouted Christian pieties. Many of the new Christian

schools did enroll a few minority students, and accurately reported that they did not have any official discriminatory bylaws. But many of them hardly recruited minority students. After Falwell and other clergy spoke out against the proposed IRS regulations, the agency dropped its threat against private schools. But Carter's reputation plummeted among white evangelicals because of the episode. Paul Weyrich recalled that the failed IRS initiative was the number one issue that galvanized white evangelicals in the 1980 election.[42]

Weyrich, Schaeffer, and others convinced Falwell to use his media and educational networks to begin the Moral Majority in 1979. Doing so came at a price for Falwell, who caught flak from fundamentalist colleagues for partnering with evangelicals, Catholics, and the small number of Jews who supported the Moral Majority. But Falwell was convinced that threats from secular humanists required cooperation with a wide range of Judeo-Christian traditionalists. Falwell insisted that pastors should address politics from the pulpit. Forming the Moral Majority freed him from tax regulations against direct political advocacy by churches. Unlike Graham, Falwell did not begin by seeking access to the top levels of power. Instead, he sought to mobilize fundamentalists and evangelicals to change the occupants of political offices. He told Christians that it was sinful not to vote. Asking pastors to hold voter registration drives, Falwell told them that they needed to get people "saved, baptized, and registered" to vote. The agenda of the Republican evangelical insiders was born.[43]

6

Evangelicalism from Reagan to Obama

The Reagan campaigns of the 1980s unified white neo-evangelicals and fundamentalists in a way they had not been since the Scopes Trial in 1925. Reagan reportedly claimed 65 and 74 percent of the evangelical vote respectively in his two presidential campaigns. Not that Reagan absolutely had to have Jerry Falwell Sr. and the Moral Majority's support. The unpopularity of Democratic candidates Jimmy Carter (1980) and Walter Mondale (1984), combined with Reagan's political genius, would likely have taken him to a two-term presidency without the help of evangelicals. Reagan and GOP leaders understood this reality. The year 1980 inaugurated four decades of Republicans affirming white evangelicals' priorities, such as school prayer or the pro-life cause. But evangelical insiders often felt there was little follow-through by the GOP. Reagan appointed few evangelicals in his administration, and he grievously disappointed pro-lifers by appointing Sandra Day O'Connor to the Supreme Court. O'Connor had a pro-choice voting record in Arizona. She became one of the court's swing votes that confirmed the constitutional right to abortion in decisions such as *Planned Parenthood v. Casey* (1992). White evangelicals were much happier with the nomination of judges such as Antonin Scalia, who became the court's most prominent conservative. But by the end of Reagan's first year in office, some frustrated Christian Right leaders were wondering whether the administration believed that they had "contributed significantly to his election" at all.[1]

In the Reagan era, not participating in partisan politics remained a live option for evangelicals (as it does today). Many evangelical and Pentecostal pastors stuck to the rule of nonpartisanship. It was hard for evangelicals ever to escape the public implications of their faith, but endorsing candidates or a party was a big step beyond commenting on issues. It was a step that many pastors remained unwilling to take. Some of America's most flamboyant televangelists of the 1980s, including the Pentecostal ministers Rex Humbard and Jimmy Swaggart, stayed out of the political fray. Day to day, the average evangelical still focused on matters such as marriage, kids, work, and the local church more than partisan politics. At least since 1980, white evangelicals have been more likely than the average American to vote. But in every presidential election year there are still about 40 percent of white evangelicals who do not vote. Not voting does not make them any less of an evangelical, except to Republican insider evangelicals who suggest that not voting is sinful. In recent years some evangelical leaders, concerned about the Moral Majority's excesses, have assured their followers that not voting is acceptable. John Piper of Desiring God Ministries, for example, said in 2016 that voting "is not a binding duty . . . for Christians in every election." Piper also announced that he would not vote for Donald Trump or Hillary Clinton.[2]

This is not to downplay the strong connection between white evangelicals and the GOP. The majority of self-identified white evangelicals since 1952 have voted in presidential elections, and they usually voted Republican. The burgeoning media culture of politicized evangelicalism aided this pattern. Evangelicals and Pentecostals had more access to Christian-friendly news, such as on Pat Robertson's television program *The 700 Club*, and on the Fox News Channel, which began airing in 1996. Fox was not tailored for white evangelicals alone, but the network catered to them and it platformed key GOP insider evangelicals. These outlets conveyed the impression that to be evangelical was to be an active Republican voter.

The politicization of evangelicals was at least indirectly aided by the traditionalist reclamation of the Southern Baptist Convention. This great denominational transformation began in 1979, when traditionalists launched the conservative resurgence. They sought to bring the largest Protestant denomination fully in line with evangelical doctrine and social views. Since 1845, the influence of southern history and regionalism had detached the SBC somewhat from its evangelical roots. Founded to defend Christian slaveholding (for which its leaders apologized in 1995), by the 1950s the SBC had become the nation's largest Protestant denomination. The SBC remained conversionist and missions-oriented, but it was self-consciously southern. The SBC did not join the National Association of Evangelicals. Foy Valentine, the head of the SBC's Christian Life Commission, spoke for many SBC moderates in 1976 when he explained that Southern Baptists "are not evangelicals. That's a Yankee word." Southern Baptists wanted nothing to do with evangelicals' "fussy fundamentalism," Valentine said. Leaders such as Valentine figured there was room in their big denomination for theological variety, especially on issues not related to salvation. Though they might be personally conservative, SBC moderates were not interested in what Valentine called "theological witch-hunts."[3]

SBC conservatives were committed to the Bible's inerrancy, a doctrine that many moderates saw as divisive. Conservatives believed that the SBC seminaries had become infiltrated by theological liberals. This divide precipitated a feud that harked back to the fundamentalist-modernist fights of the early 1900s. The SBC had some troubles in those days, such as the controversy over modernist Crawford Toy at Southern Baptist Theological Seminary. But the SBC had seen nothing like the war that started in 1979.

Conservatives Paige Patterson and Judge Paul Pressler figured that if they could control the SBC presidency for a decade, they could bring all SBC schools and agencies under their sway. Because Baptists practice congregational autonomy, it was more difficult to commandeer individual churches. But conservatives hoped that theological uniformity in seminaries would trickle down to local congregations. The conservative plan began with the election of Memphis pastor Adrian Rogers as SBC president in 1979. A host of cultural and scriptural issues animated conservatives, including opposition to ordaining women pastors. (New Testament passages such as I Timothy 2–3 and I Corinthians 14:34–35 suggested to conservatives that the Bible did not permit women to hold senior pastoral positions.) All these issues ultimately centered around the authority of the Bible. W. A. Criswell addressed the SBC in 1985, the meeting that saw the decisive election of the resurgence. Criswell proclaimed that "if the higher critical approach to scriptures dominates our institutions and our denomination," the SBC's historic commitment to evangelism would fall away. "There will be no missionaries to hurt. They will cease. . . . Whether we continue to live or ultimately die lies in our dedication to the infallible Word of God."[4]

By the late 1980s, SBC conservatives began replacing faculty and other denominational officials with inerrantists, a policy that sometimes created ugly scenes at the seminaries. When trustees fired Russell Dilday as president of Southwestern Baptist Theological Seminary in Fort Worth in 1994, the locks on his office door were changed within minutes.[5] This is a common practice in American business, but the episode engendered bitterness among moderates that lingered for decades. Dilday was not theologically liberal, but he was critical of the conservatives' tactics. He was comfortable with having some liberals at the seminary. Patterson, a protégé of W. A. Criswell and onetime president of Criswell College in Dallas, would become the president of Southwestern himself in 2003. His term ended in 2018 as a result of allegations that he had mishandled sexual assault charges and made insensitive comments about women.

Changes at Southern Baptist Theological Seminary in Louisville were representative of the SBC's wholesale transformation. Albert Mohler became president of Southern Seminary in 1993. Mohler admired Carl Henry (who died in 2003) and his combination of cultural engagement and theological traditionalism. Mohler brought Southern's faculty in line with inerrancy and opposition to women's ordination. Mohler also sought to restore an older Baptist commitment to Calvinism that had fallen out of favor since the Civil War. This included beliefs such as limited or definite atonement, or the idea that Christ died only for the sins of the elect, not for all of humankind. Within a few years, virtually the whole faculty at Southern had resigned or been removed. Those who departed included some genuine liberals, but also some professors who affirmed inerrancy but supported women's ordination.[6]

In 2004, Mohler named Russell Moore as dean of the School of Theology at Southern. Moore would become president of the SBC's Ethics and Religious Liberty Commission in 2013. In that role, Moore has emerged as one of the most articulate defenders of evangelical views of culture and church. He also cautions white evangelicals to be wary of the excesses of the Moral Majority. Moore, Mohler, and other conservative SBC leaders identify with the broader evangelical community in ways that Foy Valentine's generation did not. Mohler and Moore have both served on the leadership council of The Gospel Coalition, a popular Reformed and evangelical website that includes conservative pastors from a range of denominations and ethnic backgrounds. Consciously drawing on evangelical history, Mohler and Moore position themselves in the tradition of leaders such as Carl Henry, who was only marginally connected to the SBC.[7]

Architects of the conservative resurgence hoped that the SBC could avoid the decline of the mainline denominations. These denominations—such as the U.S. Episcopal Church and the United Methodist Church—entered a catastrophic era of plummeting membership starting in the 1960s. Some evangelicals remained within most of these denominations, but modernists generally controlled their leadership and seminaries. In light of the slow-motion mainline collapse, many evangelicals crowed that theological liberalism was a sure cause of church decay. Presumably, theological orthodoxy would stave it off. But by the mid-2010s it became clear that the SBC also had entered a pattern of dwindling baptisms and membership, though not a decline as severe as the mainline churches experienced. From its high mark of 16.3 million reported members in 2003, the SBC had dropped to 15.2 million in 2016. It remains to be seen whether a flurry of new SBC church plants will counter that trend.[8]

Other evangelical denominations were growing, however. The Presbyterian Church in America (PCA), a Reformed traditionalist 1974 breakaway from the mainline Presbyterian Church USA, grew from 67,000 members in 1975 to 360,000 in 2013. However, statistics from 2015 to 2017 suggested that PCA growth had also leveled off. The PCA is the denomination of Redeemer Presbyterian Church in Manhattan, where until 2017 Timothy Keller was senior pastor. Keller, like Russell Moore, helped evangelicals project a more urbane, intellectual style while adhering to biblicist and conversionist theology. Keller has largely avoided partisan politics and prefers the term "orthodox" to describe himself rather than evangelical. Keller realizes that it is hard to escape the Republican connotations of the term evangelical, connotations that would not serve his church well in largely liberal New York City. The strength of the PCA, and the popularity of Keller, Moore, Mohler, John Piper, and others, illustrates the flourishing of Calvinist and Reformed theology among evangelicals in recent decades. That flourishing has been complemented by schools such as Southern Baptist Theological Seminary and the PCA-affiliated Reformed Theological Seminary, which has a number of campuses and extensions, mainly in the South. Popular teaching ministries such as the late R. C. Sproul's Ligonier Ministries, John Piper's Desiring God, and The Gospel Coalition have also introduced Reformed theology to broad evangelical audiences.[9]

Pentecostal churches are generally the fastest-growing denominations among Protestants. The Church of God in Christ, for example, has gone from 425,000 reported members in 1965 to 6.5 million in sixty-three countries today. The Assemblies of God (AG) went from 572,000 members in 1965 to 3.2 million in the U.S. alone in 2015. Most of the AG growth has been among nonwhites. And much of the recent increase among AG whites has been among immigrants from eastern Europe.[10]

By the 2010s, the AG was nearly a "majority minority" denomination, in which nonwhites make up more than half of the members. AG increases have been especially strong among Hispanics. By the mid-2010s, the AG had seven hundred thousand Latino adherents. The key AG leader in Hispanic ministry in the late twentieth century was Jesse Miranda. Miranda's devotion to the Pentecostal church began when, as a boy, he saw his mother healed by her congregation's prayers. Miranda eventually received a D.Min. from Fuller Seminary and founded the Alianza de Ministerios Evangélicos Nacionales (AMEN) as an interdenominational clearinghouse for voicing Latino evangelical views. Presidents from Ronald Reagan to Barack Obama consulted with Miranda on issues relevant to the Latino community. In 2006, AMEN merged with the National Hispanic Christian Leadership Conference (NHCLC). Under the leadership of Samuel Rodriguez, who is also ordained in the AG, the NHCLC has become the most visible advocacy group for Hispanic evangelicals. Among Latinos, the word *evangélicos* tends to accord with the deeper historical meaning of the term as "non-Catholics."[11]

Latino Pentecostals blend evangelism and social ministry as they reconcile the "message of Billy Graham with the activism of Martin Luther King Jr.," as Rodriguez puts it. Latino evangelical leaders and the NHCLC have sought influence and access, but they have been less beholden to one party than white evangelicals. Thus, some NHCLC leaders—including Chicago megachurch pastor Wilfredo "Choco" de Jesús—supported President Obama in 2008, while Rodriguez prayed at Donald Trump's 2016 inauguration. Rodriguez has also criticized Trump, especially for his views on immigration and failure to support the DACA (Deferred Action for Childhood Arrivals) program for the children of undocumented immigrants.[12]

The NHCLC reflects a longtime trend among evangelicals to organize across denominational lines (although the NHCLC is dominated by pastors who have an AG background). This interdenominational tendency goes back to George Whitefield, who worked with Baptists, Presbyterians, and Congregationalists, to the consternation of leaders in his own Anglican denomination. Evangelicals continue to raise up influential Bible teachers and evangelists in the line of Whitefield, Moody, McPherson, and Graham, whose ministries transcend denomination and congregation. Samuel Rodriguez is one of today's examples of this. He is known for his work with the NHCLC, and his Twitter account links to the website pastorsam.com, where you can also find information about the church he pastors in Sacramento.

Evangelicals in recent decades have embraced the work of evangelists such as Luis Palau and the Indian-born apologist Ravi Zacharias. But since the 1980s popular Bible teachers, not evangelists, have been more likely to capture the attention of core evangelicals. Like the great evangelists of the past, prominent Bible teachers employ the latest styles of communication—now including social media—to spread their message. Three contemporary examples of such teachers are Tony Evans, Beth Moore, and John Piper. Each of these figures is connected to a local church, but they speak to far bigger evangelical audiences. Each is primarily a teacher of believers rather than an evangelist to the unconverted.

Evans is the pastor of Oak Cliff Bible Fellowship, a megachurch in Dallas with more than ten thousand members. Evans was the first African American to receive a doctorate from

Dallas Theological Seminary (DTS), the twentieth century's institutional home of dispensational theology, a system of evangelical doctrine that influenced popular views about the last days before Christ's return. (The phenomenally popular end-times writer Hal Lindsey graduated from DTS.) In 1976, Evans founded a home church with ten people that became Oak Cliff Bible Fellowship. Evans became nationally known through his radio program *The Alternative* (formerly *The Urban Alternative*), which plays on twelve hundred radio stations in the U.S. and in more than 130 countries. He has also served as chaplain for Dallas's NFL and NBA teams. Evans's church is known for innovative social programs for the poor, especially in the Oak Cliff neighborhood. His ministry reportedly influenced George W. Bush's ideas about "compassionate conservatism" and faith-based social service.[13]

Beth Moore founded Living Proof Ministries in 1994, working under the auspices of Houston's First Baptist Church for fifteen years before affiliating with Bayou City Fellowship (pastored by her son-in-law) in 2011. In 2010, *Christianity Today* declared that Moore was "the most popular Bible teacher in America." By then, more than 650,000 women had attended Moore's conferences, and millions more had read her books. As of mid-2018, she had more than 870,000 followers on Twitter. Moore's style is unmistakably Baptist and southern, but she reaches an international evangelical audience. Moore has spoken frankly about her experiences of enduring abuse as a child and has become one of evangelical culture's fiercest critics for its tolerance of abuse and misogyny. Although she was careful not to name him directly, in 2016 Moore criticized white evangelicals who supported Donald Trump after the *Access Hollywood* video surfaced in which Trump bragged about accosting women. Moore is an unusual figure in evangelical circles, a female Bible teacher whose husband is in the background of her ministry. But she's not alone—Jen Wilkin of the SBC-affiliated Village Church (in the Dallas area) is another example of a popular theologically conservative female Bible teacher. Moore and Wilkin both appeal primarily to female audiences, however.[14]

Finally, John Piper, former pastor of Bethlehem Baptist Church in Minneapolis, has turned Desiring God Ministries into one of the most influential voices in evangelical culture. Piper is a native southerner, but he encountered the wider world of evangelicalism when he attended Chicago-area Wheaton College in the mid-1960s. He did graduate work at Fuller Seminary and earned a doctorate from the University of Munich. For six years, Piper taught biblical studies at Bethel College, a Christian college in St. Paul, Minnesota, affiliated with the Baptist General Conference (a denomination now called Converge). In 1980 Piper became pastor of Bethlehem Baptist Church. Piper was especially influenced by the writings of Jonathan Edwards and C. S. Lewis, a mid-twentieth-century Anglican writer who is a favorite of many American evangelicals. Drawing on themes in Edwards and Lewis, Piper burst onto the national evangelical scene with his 1986 book *Desiring God: Meditations of a Christian Hedonist*. In it, Piper argued that the aim of the Christian life was to find fulfillment and joy in knowing God.

Piper also became known as a champion of "complementarianism," the idea that women and men have distinct, biblically defined roles in marriage and in the church. Piper reflected a renewed emphasis on complementarianism among Baptists and many other evangelicals, especially as women's ordination became more accepted in mainline denominations. Inspired by the conservative resurgence, the SBC's updated versions of the 1998 and 2000 Baptist Faith and Message said that a married woman should "submit herself graciously to the servant leadership of her husband," and it limited the pastoral office to men. (The submission statement derived from New Testament passages such as Ephesians 5:22.) Evangelicals are hardly the only Christians to exclude women from the pastoral office: Catholics and Orthodox Christians have much longer traditions of exclusively male clergy. Some Pentecostals have been more open to women in pastoral roles than other evangelicals, with married Pentecostal co-pastors being a common arrangement. But some moderate evangelicals such as Bill Hybels of Willow Creek Community Church in Chicago have defended the "egalitarian" view that all church offices should be equally open to women and men.[15]

In 1994, Piper founded Desiring God, which has become one of the largest evangelical teaching ministries and has a major online presence. By mid-2018, Piper had almost a million followers on Twitter, though this falls short of other American religious leaders such as Saddleback Church's Rick Warren with 2.4 million, and the cheerful prosperity gospel preacher Joel Osteen with 8.6 million.

Contemporary evangelicalism retains links to its past. The most prominent continuities include an interdenominational impulse, an emphasis on God's discernible presence, struggles over questions of race and gender, and the desire to foster revival and to send out missionaries. Bible teaching, missions sending, and other defining evangelical practices rarely make it into the news. News understandably thrives on controversy, especially political controversy. Thus, since the 1980 election the public image of white evangelicals has been dominated by the work of the Republican insiders. Many polls about evangelicals allow a category only for whites. This means that "evangelical" is often coded directly as "white" in the news, in spite of the racial diversity within evangelical and Pentecostal ranks. "Black Protestants" are often given a separate category, while Hispanic Protestants sometimes get no category at all.[16] Many surveys also depend upon self-identification alone in order to identify evangelicals or the born again. This methodology leaves a host of unanswered questions about respondents' beliefs, their rate of church attendance, and whether "evangelical," to them, is more of a political and ethnic designation than a religious marker.[17]

Like many Republicans, the evangelical insiders look back nostalgically at Ronald Reagan's two terms as a golden age. This remains the case even though Reagan was more of "an evangelical's president than an evangelical president," as historian Steven Miller puts it. Reagan was staunchly anticommunist. He spoke in providential terms about America. Reagan repeatedly cited John Winthrop's (and Jesus's) "city upon a hill" metaphor, applying it to the United States. America had fallen away from its God-given calling in the 1960s and 1970s, Reagan suggested, but anticommunist resolve and economic empowerment through tax cuts would put the nation back on the right track. "Let's make America great again," Reagan posters and buttons declared, a phrase that Donald Trump would make the centerpiece of his 2016 campaign.[18]

Most Republican evangelicals were comfortable with the presidential model pioneered by Dwight Eisenhower: a Republican anticommunist who was respectful of Christianity, even if not personally devout. That model had worked for Nixon and Reagan, though Nixon's criminal duplicity temporarily threw the white evangelical/Republican union into turmoil. The year 1988 saw another moment of uncertainty for Republican evangelical insiders. George H. W. Bush was no evangelical, and he

was not good at acting like one. Even though Reagan's vice
president was one of the most seasoned candidates ever to run
for president, some evangelical partisans went looking elsewhere. Some rallied around New York congressman Jack Kemp,
an articulate champion of free-market economics. But Christian
Broadcasting Network's Pat Robertson wanted to lead Christian
conservatives out of their marginal position and become
president himself. To the dismay of many fundamentalist-
leaning evangelicals (including Jerry Falwell), Robertson was a
Pentecostal who routinely received prophetic "words of knowledge" (based on I Corinthians 12:8). Words of knowledge and
prayers for divine healings were regular features of his *700 Club*
show. Nevertheless, Robertson's surprising success in the GOP
primaries, including a second-place finish in the Iowa caucuses,
was one of the highest achievements ever for the Republican
insider evangelicals. One of their own had finally, if ephemer-
ally, become a contender for the Republican nomination.[19]

The years from 1988 to 2000 found Republican insiders in
a wilderness time, however. Largely excluded from influence in
George H. W. Bush's administration, white evangelicals were
even more dismayed by Bill Clinton's election. Like his fellow
Baptist Jimmy Carter, Clinton was comfortable talking about
faith. Billy Graham prayed at both of Clinton's inaugurations,
reflecting Graham's increasingly bipartisan stance. In spite of his
signing the Defense of Marriage Act, which allowed states not
to recognize gay marriages, Clinton did not employ his faith in
policy directions that most evangelical whites found acceptable.
His veto of a bill that would have made partial birth abortion
illegal won Clinton the special animus of evangelical activists.
Even left-leaning white evangelicals such as Ron Sider's Evangelicals for Social Action criticized Clinton for his permissiveness
on abortion.[20]

After Reagan's reelection in 1984, funding for the Moral Majority and other Christian Right groups dropped significantly. Jerry Falwell Sr. increasingly drew scorn from the Left, not least when he visited the white supremacist bastion of South Africa in 1985 and returned advising Christians to invest in the country. He said that he was opposed to racial apartheid in South Africa, but Falwell was also worried about a communist insurgency taking over the country if the U.S. dropped its support. (William Bentley, former head of the National Black Evangelical Association, mused that Falwell's gradualist approach to ending apartheid was predictable because "people who control the segregation process always say 'wait.'")[21] When Falwell stepped down from the Moral Majority, it took the remaining momentum out of the organization, which dissolved in 1989.

Pat Robertson's Christian Coalition, led by the savvy Republican operative Ralph Reed, stepped into the breach left by the Moral Majority. Reed showed Republicans how to do evangelical outreach at the local level. Clinton's presidency energized the Christian Coalition, which placed supporters in leadership positions throughout the Republican Party and partnered with congressional Republicans such as House Speaker Newt Gingrich. It was not always clear why white evangelicals should have a special affinity for the anti-Clinton Republicans, however. Gingrich's signature platform, the 1994 Contract with America, said little about social issues such as abortion and school prayer.[22]

Gary Bauer, the head of James Dobson's Family Research Council, emerged as another key evangelical organizer. Bauer sought to expand upon Pat Robertson's example by running in the Republican primaries in 2000. But Bauer's candidacy was short-circuited by the emergence of Texas governor George W. Bush as a preferred choice of white evangelicals. Bush projected a certain coolness toward evangelicals, as his father had. But the younger Bush still resonated with religious conservatives because he had an honest-to-goodness evangelical "testimony." This was something that Eisenhower, Nixon, and George H. W. Bush did not have. Reagan vaguely alluded to such a testimony, and Jimmy Carter had one but his politics negated its significance for Republican evangelicals.

George W. Bush, by contrast, had a personal story of stark moral transformation. As a hard-partying rich young man, he developed a dependence on alcohol that threatened his career and marriage. He prayed to accept Christ in 1984, and then had a meaningful talk about following Jesus with Billy Graham in 1985. He preferred to emphasize the latter conversation when publicly recounting his testimony. Although Bush avoided the term "born again," he made it clear that Jesus had changed his "heart," as he related in a 1999 Republican debate. "When you turn your heart and your life over to Christ, when you accept Christ as the savior," he explained, "it changes your heart, it changes your life, and that's what happened to me."[23] Republican evangelicals couldn't ask for more.

Bush's testimony, in addition to his political credentials and folksy charm, made him an ideal choice for Republican evangelicals. Bush desperately needed their help in the 2000 election. In spite of losing the national popular vote to Al Gore, Bush eked out a bitter victory in Florida and won the Electoral College. Bush advisor Karl Rove, a nominal Episcopalian and rumored agnostic, took detailed lessons from Ralph Reed's model of evangelical mobilization. Wanting to avoid the narrow outcome of 2000, Rove made the most systematic effort ever to get white evangelicals to the polls in 2004. Bush also delivered some substantial if politically safe victories to Christian conservatives, including signing the 2003 Partial-Birth Abortion Act. He created the White

House Office of Faith-Based and Community Initiatives, inspired by Bush's fondness for compassionate conservatism.

Still, attention to the Republican evangelicals' domestic agenda was inconsistent, especially after the 9/11 attacks made anti-terrorism the administration's central priority. For many Republicans and their evangelical allies, the "war on terror" functioned as a substitute for anticommunism in the decades following the Soviet Union's collapse. The leadership of the Republican insider evangelicals was transitioning, too. Jerry Falwell Sr. struck a discordant note on Robertson's *700 Club* shortly after 9/11, saying that gays and those in favor of abortion had elicited the judgment of God on America. This was strong providentialist stuff, not something that even most militant evangelical Republicans were willing to affirm.[24]

Billy Graham, still seen by many as "America's Pastor," spoke at the National Day of Prayer service in the days following 9/11. But as Billy aged, his son Franklin became more prominent. Franklin Graham was the longtime president of the global charity Samaritan's Purse, and he preached at evangelistic events for the Billy Graham Association. Franklin Graham still projected a relatively nonpartisan profile when he prayed at George W. Bush's inauguration in 2001, though both Graham and Houston megachurch pastor Kirbyjon Caldwell generated controversy at that ceremony by insisting upon praying in Jesus's name. Franklin Graham, however, made news by denouncing Islam as an "evil and wicked religion" after 9/11. This departed from President Bush, who insisted that true Islam was a religion of peace. Many evangelical insiders such as the younger Graham wanted Republicans to take a harsher stance on Islam than Bush did.[25] This desire helps account for the solid white evangelical support (including Franklin Graham's) for Donald Trump in 2016.

In addition to his moderation on Muslims, George W. Bush would not fully support a constitutional amendment affirming heterosexual marriage. The legal status of gay marriage was arguably the top issue for the evangelical Republicans from about 2003 until the *Obergefell v. Hodges* decision (2015), which required states to license gay marriages. Unlike *Roe v. Wade*, which precipitated a long-lasting pro-life movement, *Obergefell* appears to have ended substantial attempts to counter gay marriage through legislation or amendment. The decision seems likely to have been the last judicial word on the question. Donald Trump rarely commented on the issue in 2016, expressing some concern about *Obergefell* but seeming to accept the decision.

Whatever their growing frustrations in 2004 with Bush on social issues, politically active white evangelicals felt they had nowhere else to turn. The secular-minded Democrat John Kerry was hardly acceptable to them. Rove was able to get 3 million more self-identified evangelicals to vote for Bush in 2004 than in 2000. Evangelical Republicans were generally pleased when Bush nominated John Roberts for the Supreme Court, but Bush's 2005 nomination of White House counsel Harriet Miers was a debacle. Miers's personal views on abortion and marriage were largely unknown. Scant evidence suggested that she might have been pro-choice and pro–gay rights as recently as the 1990s. Miers ultimately withdrew her candidacy and was replaced by the solidly conservative justice Samuel Alito. The Miers episode, however, illustrated again the tenuousness of Republican evangelicals' strategy to elect presidents who would appoint pro-life judges. Repeated disappointments on that score included Sandra Day O'Connor and the liberal George H. W. Bush appointee David Souter. Still, one of the most constant refrains of the evangelical insiders is the need to vote Republican for the sake of the Supreme Court.[26]

George W. Bush had arguably the most ideal Christian profile of any GOP nominee ever, yet even he proved vaguely disappointing to Republican evangelical insiders because of his lukewarm approach to key social issues. The next three Republican nominees were even less appealing. The combative Arizona senator John McCain had brawled with Falwell Sr. and Robertson during the 2000 primaries, calling them "agents of intolerance" as his campaign faltered. To heal that feud in the run-up to 2008, McCain spoke at Falwell's Liberty University. McCain also took to saying that the Constitution "establishes a Christian nation." That assertion might appear implausible in light of the no-establishment clause of the First Amendment and the Constitution's relative silence about God. But the idea that America is, in some sense, a Christian nation is a perennial claim of the Republican evangelical activists. The Christian nation thesis has been promoted by Republican operatives such as the popular evangelical history writer David Barton.

The year 2008 also saw prosperity gospel preachers and televangelists such as Rod Parsley and John Hagee emerge as key Republican Christian activists. Though many evangelicals had serious reservations about prosperity theology (and, to a lesser extent, Hagee's and Parsley's exotically detailed prophetic teachings about Israel), the media had little interest in Parsley's and Hagee's beliefs except to the extent that they caused problems for McCain. McCain ultimately distanced himself from both figures when anti-Muslim statements and other embarrassing comments by Hagee and Parsley came to light, although McCain himself had questioned American Muslims' ability to fit within the nation's political tradition. McCain's erratic courtship of evangelical Republicans culminated with his choice of Alaska governor Sarah Palin as running mate. Palin had a deep background in Pentecostalism. Reluctant evangelicals such as James Dobson were persuaded to support McCain because of Palin. Self-identified white evangelicals overwhelmingly supported McCain, but it was not enough to turn the election in his favor.[27]

Barack Obama's presidency signaled another wilderness season for the Republican insiders. Obama courted moderate evangelical leaders such as Rick Warren, who hosted a 2008 discussion at Saddleback Church with McCain and Obama. Warren prayed at Obama's inauguration, to the chagrin of LGBT activists, who deplored Warren's support for traditional marriage. LGBT activists did force the withdrawal of Atlanta pastor Louie Giglio from Obama's second inauguration. Giglio is also a moderate evangelical but affirms conservative views of sexuality. Like Bill Clinton, Obama was articulate about faith, and like George W. Bush, Obama had a clear testimony of conversion. In Obama's case, it was a conversion from skepticism to progressive Christianity. Fox News personalities including Donald Trump stoked rumors that Obama was not born in the U.S. and was not a Christian. But in his autobiography Obama told of how he came to the point where he could "walk down the aisle of Trinity United Church of Christ one day and be baptized. . . . Kneeling beneath that cross on the South Side of Chicago, I felt God's spirit beckoning me."[28] This was a mainline conversion, not an evangelical one, but it was a conversion story nonetheless. Like Clinton, however, Obama did not direct his faith convictions toward ends that suited Republican insiders.

The Republican Party was desperate to unseat President Obama in 2012. GOP evangelical insiders shared that goal, plus they wanted a nominee more reliable on social issues than McCain or George W. Bush. Early evangelical support divided among several candidates, including Texas governor Rick Perry, Senator Rick Santorum, and Congresswoman Michele

Bachmann, an evangelical who cited Francis Schaeffer as an influence. This scattering helped ensure the nomination of Mitt Romney, the telegenic former Massachusetts governor and favorite of the GOP establishment. Romney presented a unique test for the white evangelical obeisance to the Republican Party because Romney was a Mormon, the first to run as a major party nominee. Although some Mormons identify as evangelical Christians, most mainstream evangelicals reject Mormon theology and its signature text, the Book of Mormon. The Moral Majority era had softened some of the animosity between evangelicals and Mormons, in the name of political unity. But harsh criticism of Mormons endured in some fundamentalist-leaning circles. First Baptist Dallas pastor Robert Jeffress, a Rick Perry supporter, proclaimed in 2011 that Mormonism was a cult and that Mitt Romney "is not a Christian."[29]

Jeffress had become the pastor of First Baptist Dallas, W. A. Criswell's congregation, in 2007. Until 2011 he was virtually unknown outside of Texas, save for a fleeting controversy in 1998 when, as pastor of First Baptist Church of Wichita Falls, Texas, Jeffress protested a public library for owning pro-gay books. Jeffress's connection to Rick Perry provided a chance for him to garner national attention. His comments about Mormonism did the trick. They were embarrassing to Perry, who repudiated them. But Jeffress's comments earned him an appearance on the Fox News program *Fox and Friends*. Jeffress would eventually become one of Fox's most bombastic evangelical commentators. Fox had become the highest-rated cable news network in 2002, and the network could anoint the most visible Republican evangelicals simply by giving them a platform. By 2016, two of the key Fox News evangelicals were Jeffress and Franklin Graham. (Historian John Fea helpfully calls these Republican insiders the "court evangelicals.")[30] They were always ready to appear on camera with provocative statements about Democrats, Muslims, and other groups. After failing to secure the GOP nomination in 2008, former Baptist pastor and Arkansas governor Mike Huckabee even got his own variety show on Fox before moving to the prosperity gospel–dominated Trinity Broadcasting Network in 2017.

Jeffress and most other white evangelical voters did support Romney in the general election, especially after the Obama administration promulgated the 2012 Health and Human Services mandate, which required that organizations, including faith-based ones, provide employee coverage for contraceptives and abortifacients. Romney ended up receiving roughly the same amount of support from white evangelicals as George W. Bush did in 2004. This wasn't enough, and President Obama handily won a second term.

By 2016, white evangelicals' engagement with politics ran along familiar lines. Many evangelicals were not engaged with partisan politics, of course, and those who were had exceedingly diverse views of politics, especially depending upon their ethnicity. But white evangelicals who quixotically sought power in the GOP had come to represent evangelicalism itself for much of the American public. It would be easy to blame the media for this phenomenon. Much of the media cares about religion only to the extent that religion is connected to scandal, politics, or conflict. But GOP evangelical insiders have also supplied a ready-made narrative of their quest for influence, a quest that has stayed roughly consistent since Dwight Eisenhower's presidency. White evangelical activists' union with the GOP has arguably brought few results on issues that evangelicals care about most. Pro-lifers have made only episodic legislative or judicial progress since *Roe v. Wade*. And the battle to stop gay marriage likely suffered permanent defeat in the *Obergefell* decision.

Nevertheless, white evangelical support for the GOP has endured. That fealty met its greatest test ever in 2016. The 2016 presidential election would become the most shattering experience for evangelicals since the Scopes Trial.

Coda

Donald Trump and the Crisis of Evangelicalism

In 2016, Donald Trump scooped up endorsements from Republican evangelical insiders such as Franklin Graham, Robert Jeffress, and Jerry Falwell Jr. Trump carefully cultivated the support of evangelical insiders, religious Fox News contributors, and prosperity gospel preachers. A key moment in Trump's courtship of evangelicals came in January 2016, when he spoke at Liberty University. Trump's speech stumbled on a couple points as he uttered some mild profanities and referred to the New Testament book of "Two Corinthians" instead of the conventional "Second Corinthians."[1] Falwell (who took over as Liberty's president in 2007) said that Trump was "one of the greatest visionaries of our time" and that "Mr. Trump lives a life of loving and helping others as Jesus taught in the New Testament." In June 2016, Falwell tweeted a picture of himself and his wife Becki posing next to Trump in the businessman's office. A framed cover of the soft-core pornographic *Playboy* featuring Trump hung on the wall.

Many black-led Protestant churches seemed as committed to Hillary Clinton's candidacy as white evangelicals were to Trump's. By late summer 2016, almost 30 percent of attendees at African American congregations had heard their pastor speak positively about Clinton, in spite of IRS rules forbidding pastors from endorsing candidates.[2] One of Hillary Clinton's last stops of her ill-fated campaign was a Church of God in Christ congregation in Philadelphia.

Political commitments based on denomination and ethnicity: this is a standard media narrative about religion in contemporary America. There are alternative perspectives, however, for those interested in seeing them. Many white evangelical leaders—even ones typically quiet about partisan politics—expressed grave reservations about Donald Trump in 2016, especially after the emergence of the infamous *Access Hollywood* video. Plenty of left-leaning evangelical leaders opposed Trump, of course, but what was especially striking was the number of conservative evangelical leaders who opposed or voiced deep concern about Trump. These included Beth Moore of Living Proof Ministries, Albert Mohler and Russell Moore of the Southern Baptist Convention, John Piper of Desiring God Ministries, Marvin Olasky of *WORLD* magazine, and a number of writers affiliated with The Gospel Coalition (where I blog). Yet 81 percent of self-identified white evangelical voters supported Trump, according to some polls. Something had apparently broken in the white evangelical movement.

Black Protestants reportedly supported Clinton as a more cohesive bloc (88 percent) than white evangelicals supported Trump, although African American support for Clinton was weaker than for Barack Obama in 2008 or 2012. Few African American religious leaders registered approval of Trump. One of the most influential who did was A. R. Bernard, a Brooklyn

megachurch pastor who converted under the ministry of
Puerto Rican evangelist Nicky Cruz. Even Bernard resigned
from Trump's evangelical advisory board, however, in the wake
of controversial comments Trump made about a white supremacist rally in August 2017.[3]

Some black evangelical and Pentecostal leaders did express
concerns about Hillary Clinton. Perhaps the most notable
instance was an "Open Letter" to Clinton signed by African
American clergy and by Jacqueline Rivers, a Harvard lecturer
and the director of the Seymour Institute for Black Church
and Policy Studies. Among the signatories was Charles Blake,
the presiding bishop of the Church of God in Christ. The
letter criticized Clinton for ignoring issues of importance to
black Christians, including abortion and what they called a
"well-financed war . . . being waged by the gay and lesbian community in the US and abroad on the faith of our ancestors."[4]
Ethnicity remained a powerful indicator in 2016 for how traditional Protestants would vote. But some conservative Protestants have shown a willingness to break with those ethnic
voting patterns.

From Eisenhower to Romney, white evangelical voters had
supported Republican candidates who seemed to model personal dignity and respect for religion, even if they did not have
evangelical bona fides. At times Republican evangelicals have
been credulous about Republican candidates, especially Richard
Nixon. But 2016 found white evangelicals in a different mode.
The profane Trump gloried in a personal history that openly
contradicted evangelical standards of sexual behavior and
marital fidelity, and based much of his campaign on tough
national policy against immigrants from Central America and
the Muslim world. His 1990 appearance on the cover of *Playboy*

was illustrative of his personal traits, yet self-identifying white evangelical voters maintained their obeisance to the GOP.

How did the white evangelical alliance with Trump come to pass? Mostly it repeated evangelicals' near-automatic performance in elections since 1952: the majority of white evangelical voters have supported the GOP candidate, whoever he might be. Yes, Trump broke the mold of conventional Republican nominees by openly bragging about his history of marital infidelity and other immoral behavior. But he also showed enough attention to evangelical and Pentecostal leaders to convince them, as leaders from Eisenhower to Reagan had convinced them, that he took them seriously. Trump had once described himself as "very pro-choice," but like Mitt Romney, Trump professed to have changed his mind about abortion and become pro-life. Abortion is the single most important issue to many white evangelical voters. The first years of Trump's presidency gave backers little reason to doubt his commitment to the pro-life cause, especially when he nominated Neil Gorsuch and Brett Kavanaugh to the Supreme Court. (Because of the conventional unwillingness of nominees to comment on prospective cases, it remained unclear whether either Gorsuch or Kavanaugh would actually vote to overturn *Roe v. Wade*.) Evangelicals already knew what they would get from the staunchly pro-choice Hillary Clinton, who supported women's freedom to get even late-term abortions. Although such procedures are rare, the issue of late-term abortions has often become a test question for whether Democratic candidates would consider any restrictions on abortion rights. For many white evangelicals, there was no question about what to do on Election Day 2016, whatever their level of dissatisfaction with Trump.

In the Republican primaries, there also was a dispersion of evangelical support, as had occurred in previous election cycles.

While some, like Jeffress and Falwell Jr., were early Trump endorsers, some Moral Majority–era stalwarts such as James Dobson and Tony Perkins of the Family Research Council endorsed
Texas senator Ted Cruz. Florida senator Marco Rubio's religion
and pro-life advisory boards included evangelical and Pentecostal figures such as Saddleback Church's Rick Warren, the National Hispanic Christian Leadership Conference's Samuel
Rodriguez, Assemblies of God General Superintendent George
O. Wood, and Southern Baptist Theological Seminary president
Albert Mohler. (I was also a member of Rubio's religious
liberty advisory board.) But white and Republican-leaning Hispanic evangelicals failed to coalesce around a single candidate,
aiding Trump's improbable emergence from a large field of GOP
contenders.

The fact that many women and people of color regarded
Trump as a misogynist and racist gave some white evangelicals
pause. A conspicuous, if small, evangelical #NeverTrump movement emerged, but that movement gained traction mostly
among evangelicals who do not have much access to insider
Republican circles and Fox News. #NeverTrump appears not
to have made much impact among politically engaged, white
evangelical laypeople. In the end, #NeverTrump advocacy was
not enough to significantly reduce overall evangelical votes for
Trump.

This was a grievous disappointment to many traditionalist Christians, especially women and people of color. It generated memories of white evangelical passivity in the eras of
lynching and civil rights. Pastor Thabiti Anyabwile of Anacos-
tia River Church in Washington, D.C., wrote after the election
at The Gospel Coalition website that evangelical Trump voters
had "abandoned public solidarity with groups who considered
Mr. Trump an existential threat to them. I'm speaking here of

the many groups who expressed reservation regarding Mr. Trump's racism, religious bigotry, misogyny, isolationism, and nativism. People with those concerns came from a lot of groups in the country, including African-American Christians, many themselves evangelicals. . . . That voting decision will likely put a deep chill on efforts at reconciliation. . . . Coming back from that may be difficult."[5]

Eighty-one percent. The damage caused by evangelical white voters' support for Trump was substantial, leading many women and people of color to question the fundamental integrity of the movement. In the aftermath of the election, stories proliferated about blacks, Hispanics, and other people leaving evangelical churches and dropping the evangelical label. The 81 percent figure has renewed a sometimes acrimonious debate among scholars about what the term *evangelical* really means. Meanwhile, pollsters and the media have produced countless stories about how white evangelicals keep supporting Trump in the face of virtually any controversy.[6]

Hard information about the identity of the 81 percent is elusive, however. There's no question that millions of practicing white evangelicals followed the lead of Falwell Jr., Jeffress, Franklin Graham, and other evangelical endorsers of Trump in the November 2016 elections. But many questions remain. How many of these self-described white evangelicals voted *against* Hillary Clinton more than *for* Donald Trump? Do they actually admire Trump, or did they simply hope he'd make good Supreme Court appointments? (Some detailed postelection evidence suggested that many evangelical voters indeed voted for Trump in spite of his personal characteristics, supposing that he would be better on evangelical concerns like abortion and judges, or on the economy. Some simply thought he was the "lesser of two evils" when compared to Clinton.)[7] Similarly, what do these poll respondents believe about the Bible, the Holy Spirit, or about more granular theological topics such as the prosperity gospel? Typically we don't get answers to such questions in polling on religion and politics. Getting those answers would be far more expensive and labor-intensive than simply depending upon religious self-identification.

Oddities in the polling data also suggest many problems today with the category of evangelical. According to a 2017 LifeWay Research (a Southern Baptist organization) report, many of those who identify as "evangelical" don't hold traditional evangelical beliefs. When polls ask about denominational affiliation as well as evangelical self-identification, a surprising number of Catholics and even Eastern Orthodox Christians identify as evangelical, even though historically "evangelical" has always referred to a subset of Protestantism. Moreover, many self-identified evangelicals rarely go to church. A 2018 Pew Research report helpfully broke down the majority of self-identified white evangelicals into "Sunday Stalwarts," who regularly attend church, and the "God-and-Country Believers," who profess many of the same types of beliefs as the evangelical Sunday Stalwarts. But the God-and-Country Believers have limited connections to actual congregations, and they are the most likely of any religious group to hold hostile views toward immigrants.[8]

This uncertainty about identity is an essential component of today's evangelical crisis. The problems go back at least to the beginning of polling about evangelicals' partisan preferences. When *Christianity Today* and Gallup asked more probing questions in 1978 about those who self-identified as evangelicals, so many respondents did not accept evangelical attributes that the surveyors had to dramatically cut their estimate of evangelicals in the American population from 34 to 18 percent.[9]

Why do respondents with marginal evangelical characteristics say that they are, in fact, evangelicals? Presumably some intuitively understand "evangelical" as an ethnic, cultural, and political designation rather than a theological or devotional one. Some critics of evangelicals might say they're right: to such observers, "evangelical" carries as much racial and political freight as theological significance. That freight, critics would say, bolsters Trumpism.

Polling itself is in the midst of a credibility crisis, however. Response rates to polls of all kinds have plummeted in recent years, making it increasingly difficult to achieve results that pollsters once considered the minimal baseline for valid surveys. Responses, even for high-quality firms such as Pew Research, often do not exceed 10 percent. Baylor's Rodney Stark, one of the most influential sociologists in America in the past half century, notes that when he began work at Cal-Berkeley, the gold standard for survey response rates was 85 percent. Low responses are hardly the only problem: the wording of poll questions can lead to vastly different conclusions. For instance, Pew reported in 2007 that 57 percent of evangelicals believed that "many religions can lead to eternal life." LifeWay Research asked the question differently and found that only 31 percent of Protestants agreed that eternal life could come through "religions other than Christianity." Some of these evangelicals apparently meant that adherents of any religion could be saved, but *only if* they put their faith in Jesus. Polls almost always leave the *meaning* of responses open to question.[10]

Some cynics might insist that political behavior *is* what makes an evangelical an evangelical. And that is the impression left by much media coverage of evangelicals since 1976. Republican insider evangelicals, including Mike Huckabee, Franklin Graham, Robert Jeffress, and Jerry Falwell Jr., have eagerly fed the public that politicized impression in order to maintain their positions as leading evangelical spokesmen on Fox and in other venues.

However, it could be that there are positive traits that mark evangelicals more consistently than marching in lockstep with the GOP, if by "evangelical" we do not mean merely whites who self-identify as evangelical. The most obvious such trait is the evangelical penchant for charitable ministry and giving, a tendency that dates back to the founding decades of the evangelical movement and the moral reform campaigns of the nineteenth century. This is not the place to explore in detail the contemporary landscape of evangelical charity, and presumably there are many evangelicals who do spend far more time on politics than charity. Critics of white evangelicals would also say that even if they do contribute to charity, it does not make up for their backing of Trump. Still, it would be noteworthy if charitable work is a more consistent marker of evangelical behavior than Republican Party activism. Practicing religious people are strikingly active in charitable work; they are even more likely to give and serve in *nonreligious* charities than secular people are. Evangelicals are doing their part in this charitable equation.[11]

Everywhere you look on the charitable landscape, evangelicals are there. A 2017 Baylor-sponsored study showed that nearly 60 percent of all "emergency shelter" beds for the homeless are provided by faith-based organizations. (This does not count churches and other congregations that provide such services.) Among the major players in homeless relief are evangelical agencies such as the Salvation Army and the Association of Gospel Rescue Missions (AGRM). Founded in 1913, the AGRM has nearly 275 affiliated missions in North America, serving approximately 50 million meals and providing more than 20 million nights of lodging annually. It also offers addiction-recovery programs and provides clothing to the homeless. The organization sees the "practice of hospitality to the destitute as a catalyst for life transformation in Jesus."[12]

Two of the three biggest disaster-relief agencies in America are also evangelical: the Salvation Army and the Southern Baptist Convention. (The Red Cross is the third.) SBC disaster relief, which operates under its North American Mission Board, does not match the financial resources of the other two agencies, but it has the most trained volunteers (sixty-five thousand). If you look at ministry to the poor around the world, evangelical groups also maintain a powerful presence. A CBS report has noted that of the top "10 highest ranked and most popular child sponsorship charities on charitynavigator.org, eight are church-based." Child-sponsorship programs typically ask donors for a monthly gift to provide an impoverished child with clothes, food, education, and religious training at an affiliated church or school. The programs also encourage donors to write heartening letters to their sponsored children. Compassion International remains one of the largest evangelical child-sponsorship agencies, working with more than 1.8 million children in twenty-five countries.[13]

Clearly, evangelicals remain active in charitable ministry, giving, and service, even though this work rarely gets covered in the news. Charity is not an *exclusive* mark of evangelicals. But it does seem likely that charitable action is a more constant attribute of evangelicals than Republican political engagement is. As we have seen, black and white voters who hold evangelical beliefs tend to be Democratic and Republican, respectively, while Hispanic evangelicals' political allegiances are the most up for grabs of the three cohorts. But all those evangelicals have experienced similar spiritual phenomena, they embrace similar beliefs about the new birth, the Bible, and the felt presence of God, and they are more likely to give of their time and money than irreligious Americans.[14]

The crisis of evangelicalism has resulted from the widespread perception that the movement is primarily about obtaining power within the Republican Party. The politicization of evangelicals and the quest for established cultural status have historical precedents, such as the crusade to stop the teaching of evolution in the 1920s. The contemporary evangelical crisis began in the 1950s with white evangelicals' alliance with Dwight Eisenhower, Richard Nixon, and the Republican Party. To critics, white evangelical voters finally threw off the mask in 2016. They would accept *any* GOP candidate, including the crass Donald Trump, if it meant access to power.

White evangelicals' uncritical fealty to the GOP is real, and that fealty has done so much damage to the movement that it is uncertain whether the term *evangelical* can be rescued from its political and racial connotations. But as I have tried to convey in this book, there is a major gap between what much of evangelicalism entails in everyday practice and what evangelicalism appears to be in media coverage. White evangelicals such as Jeffress and Franklin Graham, and prosperity gospel preachers such as Paula White, have supplied a neatly packaged version of evangelicalism as a cohort of white Fox News–watching Republican voters who consider themselves religious. They even see Donald Trump as a key player in the reassertion of America's godly values and the restoration of a Christian cultural establishment, in spite of the ways that Trump manifestly contradicts those values in his personal life and rhetoric. Many in the media are interested only in the ways that evangelicals participate in political controversy. Therefore, at least since 1976 *evangelical* has become a code term for white religious Republicans. But evangelicalism in practice remains an ethnically and politically diverse movement focused on the new birth in Christ. The number of practicing evangelicals in America is presumably much lower than the number of self-identifying evangelicals. But practicing evangelicals are still a coherent movement animated by powerful concepts once articulated by Jonathan Edwards, Sarah Osborn, Phillis Wheatley, and many others in the era of the First Great Awakening, the time of evangelicalism's birth.

Perhaps I am naïve to hope that there remains a core of practicing, orthodox evangelicals who really do care more about salvation and spiritual matters than access to Republican power. In a sense, the tension between the spiritual and political goals of evangelicals has existed since the 1740s. Striking the right balance between eternal and worldly concerns is a common struggle for people of faith. Evangelicals carry the additional burden that their political behavior is constantly scrutinized, yet they no longer control the definition or perceived composition of their movement. Polls and media coverage centered on political behavior define evangelicalism for many Americans. Surveys commonly use self-identification to define who counts as an evangelical, a method that usually tells us more about public impressions and the political behavior of the movement than about the beliefs and spiritual habits of the interviewees. The Republican evangelical insiders have positioned themselves as the representative spokespeople for that politicized version of evangelicalism. As is so often the case in America, image is reality. But there's an older version of evangelicalism—one in continuity with the history of the movement—that still exists in America and around the world. Millions of practicing evangelical whites are part of the 81 percent. But we should not define evangelicalism by the 81 percent.

What, then, makes an evangelical an evangelical? Evangelicals' political behavior is important, and it has a troubling history. But at root, being an evangelical entails certain beliefs, practices, and spiritual experiences. Historically, evangelicals are a subset of Protestant Christians. They see conversion and personal commitment to Jesus as essential features of a true believer's life. They cherish the Bible as the divinely inspired Word of God. They believe that real Christians have a personal relationship with God, mediated by the guidance of Scripture and the power of the Holy Spirit. They aspire to act on those beliefs by praying, attending worship services, witnessing to the lost, studying the Bible, going and sending people on missions, and ministering to the "least of these." Partisan commitments have come and gone. Sometimes evangelicals have made terrible political mistakes. But conversion, devotion to an infallible Bible, and God's discernible presence are what make an evangelical an evangelical.

Notes

Introduction

1. Tobin Grant, "How the Polls Inflate Trump's Evangelical Support," *Religion News Service*, Aug. 3, 2016, https://religionnews.com/2016/08/03/how-the-polls-inflate-trumps-evangelical-vote/.

2. Among the best introductions to global evangelicalism and global Christianity are Mark Hutchinson and John Wolffe, *A Short History of Global Evangelicalism* (New York, 2012); Philip Jenkins, *The Next Christendom: The Coming of Global Christianity*, rev. ed. (New York, 2007); and Melani McAlister, *The Kingdom of God Has No Borders: A Global History of American Evangelicals* (New York, 2018).

3. Sean McGever, "The Vector of Salvation: The New Birth as (Only) the Beginning of Conversion for Wesley and Whitefield," in *Wesley and Whitefield? Wesley versus Whitefield?* ed. Ian J. Maddock (Eugene, Ore., 2018), 36.

4. See, for example, Henry Norris Bernard, *The Mental Characteristics of the Lord Jesus Christ* (London, 1888), 34.

5. T. M. Luhrmann, *When God Talks Back: Understanding the American Evangelical Relationship with God* (New York, 2012), xv.

6. Kate Bowler, *Blessed: A History of the American Prosperity Gospel* (New York, 2013), 7. Bowler's book is the best introduction to the prosperity gospel. Arlene Sánchez Walsh notes that globally, "Pentecostalism is often synonymous with the prosperity gospel/Word of Faith movement." Walsh, *Pentecostals in America* (New York, 2018), 103.

1

The Rise of Evangelicals

1. Robert Southey, *Letters from England* (1807; repr., Philadelphia, 1818), 89; Sarah Osborn, *Sarah Osborn's Collected Writings*, ed. Catherine Brekus (New Haven, Conn., 2017), xx.

2. Timothy Keller, *Center Church: Doing Balanced, Gospel-Centered Ministry in Your City* (Grand Rapids, Mich., 2012), 131.

3. Stephen J. Hamilton, *"Born Again": A Portrait and Analysis of the Doctrine of Regeneration within Evangelical Protestantism* (Bristol, Conn., 2017), 48–51.

4. Timothy George, *Theology of the Reformers*, 2nd ed. (Nashville, Tenn., 2013), 141–48.

5. Baird Tipson, *Hartford Puritanism: Thomas Hooker, Samuel Stone, and Their Terrifying God* (New York, 2015), 45–46, 240.

6. Charles Taylor, *A Secular Age* (Cambridge, Mass., 2007), 157.

7. Hamilton, *"Born Again,"* 67–68; Bruce Hindmarsh, *The Spirit of Early Evangelicalism: True Religion in a Modern World* (New York, 2018), 25–26; Johannes Wallmann, "Johann Arndt (1555–1621)," in *The Pietist Theologians*, ed. Carter Lindberg (Malden, Mass., 2005), 21.

8. A. G. Roeber, "The Waters of Rebirth: The Eighteenth Century and Transoceanic Protestant Christianity," *Church History* 79, no. 1 (Mar. 2010): 57; Ted A. Campbell, *The Religion of the Heart: A Study of European Religious Life in the Seventeenth and Eighteenth Centuries* (Columbia, S.C., 1991).

9. Hindmarsh, *Spirit of Early Evangelicalism*, 33; Julian of Norwich, *Revelations of Divine Love*, trans. Barry Windeatt (New York, 2015), 50.

10. Isaac Watts, *Hymns and Spiritual Songs*, 14th ed. (London, 1740), 159; Susan Friend Harding, *The Book of Jerry Falwell: Fundamentalist Language and Politics* (Princeton, N.J., 2001), xi.

11. Abram Van Engen, *Sympathetic Puritans: Calvinist Fellow Feeling in Early New England* (New York, 2015), 65; Thomas S. Kidd, *American Colonial History: Clashing Cultures and Faiths* (New Haven, Conn., 2016), 91–92.

12. Michael J. Crawford, *Seasons of Grace: Colonial New England's Revival Tradition in Its British Context* (New York, 1991), 22.

13. David Bebbington, *Evangelicalism in Modern Britain: A History from the 1730s to the 1980s* (London, 1989), 2–3.

14. Henry Scougal, *The Life of God in the Soul of Man*, 4th ed. (London, 1702), 97; Thomas S. Kidd, *George Whitefield: America's Spiritual Founding Father* (New Haven, Conn., 2014), 28–29.

15. George Whitefield, *A Short Account of God's Dealings with the Reverend Mr. George Whitefield* (London, 1740), 49; Hindmarsh, *Spirit of Early Evangelicalism*, 33–34.

16. Carla Gardina Pestana, "Whitefield and Empire," in *George Whitefield: Life, Context, and Legacy*, ed. Geordan Hammond and David Ceri Jones (Oxford, 2016), 86–87; Kidd, *Whitefield*, 196–97.

17. Thomas S. Kidd, *The Great Awakening: The Roots of Evangelical Christianity in Colonial America* (New Haven, Conn., 2007).

18. Jonathan Edwards, *A Faithful Narrative*, in *The Great Awakening: A Brief History with Documents*, ed. Thomas S. Kidd (Boston, 2007), 33–34.

19. Jonathan Edwards, *Religious Affections*, in *The Works of Jonathan Edwards Online*, Yale University, 203–4.

20. Osborn, *Collected Writings*, 238–39.

21. Kenneth P. Minkema, "Jonathan Edwards's Defense of Slavery," *Massachusetts Historical Review* 4 (2002): 23–59.

22. Catherine Brekus, *Sarah Osborn's World: The Rise of Evangelical Christianity in Early America* (New Haven, Conn., 2013), 287–88.

23. Kidd, *George Whitefield*, 188–90.

24. Kidd, *George Whitefield*, 215–16.

25. Kidd, *George Whitefield*, 243–44.

26. Vincent Caretta, *Phillis Wheatley: Biography of a Genius in Bondage* (Athens, Ga., 2011), 72–77; John C. Shields, *Phillis Wheatley's Poetics of Liberation: Background and Contexts* (Knoxville, Tenn., 2008), 95. On Wheatley as an evangelical, see, for instance, Caretta, *Phillis Wheatley*, 44; Brekus, *Sarah Osborn's World*, 268.

2

Evangelicals Ascendant and the Coming of the Civil War

1. Thomas S. Kidd, *God of Liberty: A Religious History of the American Revolution* (New York, 2010), 37–38.

2. Roger Williams, *Mr. Cotton's Letter Lately Printed, Examined and Answered* (1644), in *The Sacred Rights of Conscience*, ed. Daniel L. Dreisbach and Mark David Hall (Indianapolis, 2009), 147.

3. Carla Gardina Pestana, *Quakers and Baptists in Colonial Massachusetts* (New York, 1991), 32–34.

4. Thomas S. Kidd, *The Great Awakening: The Roots of Evangelical Christianity in Colonial America* (New Haven, Conn., 2007), 153–54.

5. Rhys Isaac, *The Transformation of Virginia, 1740–1790*, rev. ed. (Chapel Hill, N.C., 1999), 280.

6. John A. Ragosta, *Wellspring of Liberty: How Virginia's Religious Dissenters Helped Win the American Revolution and Secured Religious Liberty* (New York, 2010), 142–43.

7. Jon Butler, "Disestablishment as American Sisyphus," in *Turning Points in the History of American Evangelicalism*, ed. Heath W. Carter and Laura Rominger Porter (Grand Rapids, Mich., 2017), 44; R. Laurence Moore, *Touchdown Jesus: The Mixing of Sacred and Secular in American History* (Louisville, Ky., 2003), 174.

8. Kidd, *God of Liberty*, 5.

9. John Leland, *The Writings of the Late Elder John Leland*, ed. L. F. Greene (New York, 1845), 119.

10. Daniel L. Dreisbach, *Thomas Jefferson and the Wall of Separation between Church and State* (New York, 2002), 25–26.

11. Dreisbach and Hall, *Sacred Rights of Conscience*, 528.

12. Dreisbach, *Thomas Jefferson and the Wall of Separation*, 102–3; Philip Hamburger, *Separation of Church and State* (Cambridge, Mass., 2002), 422–34.

13. Joe Loconte, "Lead Us Not into Temptation: There Are Theological Reasons Why School Prayer Is a Bad Idea," *Los Angeles Times*, Feb. 14, 1995.

14. Roger Finke and Rodney Stark, *The Churching of America, 1776–2005: Winners and Losers in Our Religious Economy*, 2nd ed. (New Brunswick, N.J., 2005), 22–23.

15. Scholars debate whether "Arminian" is the appropriate term for Finney's theology. But he was certainly anti-Calvinist in his view of revival. Mark A. Noll, *America's God: From Jonathan Edwards to Abraham Lincoln* (New York, 2002), 306–8; Michael J. McClymond and Gerald R. McDermott, *The Theology of Jonathan Edwards* (New York, 2012), 610–11.

16. William L. Hiemstra, "Early Frontier Revivalism in Kentucky," *Register of the Kentucky Historical Society* 59, no. 2 (Apr. 1961): 140.

17. Dena J. Epstein, *Sinful Tunes and Spirituals: Black Folk Music to the Civil War* (Urbana, Ill., 2003), 198.

18. William Apess, *A Son of the Forest* (New York, 1829), 41, 91–92.

19. James D. Bratt, ed., *Antirevivalism in Antebellum America: A Collection of Religious Voices* (New Brunswick, N.J., 2006), 5–6. On the Restorationists' evangelical roots, see James L. Gorman, *Among the Early Evangelicals: The Transatlantic Origins of the Stone-Campbell Movement* (Abilene, Tex., 2017).

20. Edward D. Griffin, "Extract of a Letter," *Herald of Gospel Liberty*, Oct. 13, 1808, 13.

21. William R. Hutchinson, *Errand to the World: American Protestant Thought and Foreign Missions* (Chicago, 1987), 45–46.

22. Sam Haselby, *The Origins of American Religious Nationalism* (New York, 2015), 2–3. Curtis D. Johnson has called similar configurations the "formalist" and "antiformalist" evangelicals. Curtis D. Johnson, *Redeeming America: Evangelicals and the Road to Civil War* (Chicago, 1993), 7–8.

23. Haselby, *American Religious Nationalism*, 58.

24. Thomas S. Kidd, *Benjamin Franklin: The Religious Life of a Founding Father* (New Haven, Conn., 2017), 130; Frank Lambert, *"Pedlar in Divinity": George Whitefield and the Transatlantic Revivals, 1737–1770* (Princeton, N.J., 1994), 128.

25. Candy Gunther Brown, *The Word in the World: Evangelical Writing, Publishing, and Reading in America, 1789–1880* (Chapel Hill, N.C., 2004), 4, 51.

26. Brown, *Word in the World*, 74–78.

27. Andrea L. Turpin, *A New Moral Vision: Gender, Religion, and the Changing Purposes of American Higher Education, 1837–1917* (Ithaca, N.Y., 2016), 44; Tamara Plakins Thornton, *Handwriting in America: A Cultural History* (New Haven, Conn., 1996), 59.

28. Jane O'Brien, "The Time When Americans Drank All Day Long," *BBC News*, Mar. 9, 2015, https://www.bbc.com/news/magazine-31741615.

29. Timothy L. Smith, *Revivalism and Social Reform: American Protestantism on the Eve of the Civil War*, rev. ed. (Baltimore, 1980), 169–71.

30. Smith, *Revivalism and Social Reform*, 67–68; Russell E. Richey, Kenneth E. Rowe, and Jean Miller Schmidt, eds., *The Methodist Experience in America*, vol. 2 (Nashville, 2000), 292.

31. Albert J. Raboteau, *Slave Religion: The "Invisible Institution" in the Antebellum South*, rev. ed. (New York, 2004), 290.

32. Marie Tyler-McGraw, *An African Republic: Black and White Virginians in the Making of Liberia* (Chapel Hill, N.C., 2007), 63–70.

33. Paul Harvey, *Christianity and Race in the American South: A History* (Chicago, 2016), 67–68.

34. Stacey M. Robertson, *Hearts Beating for Liberty: Women Abolitionists in the Old Northwest* (Chapel Hill, N.C., 2010), 181.

35. Frederick Douglass, "The War with Mexico," in *The U.S. War with Mexico: A Brief History with Documents*, ed. Ernesto Chávez (Boston, 2008), 79.

36. Molly Oshatz, *Slavery and Sin: The Fight against Slavery and the Rise of Liberal Protestantism* (New York, 2012), 58–59.

37. *Report of Debates in the General Conference of the Methodist Episcopal Church* (New York, 1844), 95.

3
The "Fundamentalists" and Evangelical Controversy

1. Grace Brown Elmore, *Heritage of Woe: The Civil War Diary of Grace Brown Elmore, 1861–1868*, ed. Marli F. Weiner (Athens, Ga., 1997), 119.

2. William R. Hutchinson, *The Modernist Impulse in American Protestantism* (Durham, N.C., 1992), 114. On the definition of mainline Protestantism, see Elesha J. Coffman, *The Christian Century and the Rise of the Protestant Mainline* (New York, 2013), 4–6.

3. Thomas S. Kidd and Barry Hankins, *Baptists in America: A History* (New York, 2015), 153; William E. Montgomery, *Under Their Own Vine and Fig Tree: The African-American Church in the South, 1865–1900* (Baton Rouge, La., 1993), 108–11.

4. *Baptist Home Missions in North America* (New York, 1883), 486–87; Kidd and Hankins, *Baptists in America*, 121.

5. Leandro Fernandez to Thomas Harwood, June 18, 1909, in Thomas Harwood, *History of New Mexico Spanish and English Missions of the Methodist Episcopal Church* (Albuquerque, N.M., 1910), 4; Juan Francisco Martínez, *The Story of Latino Protestants in the United States* (Grand Rapids, Mich., 2018), 38–39.

6. James F. Findlay, *Dwight L. Moody: American Evangelist, 1837–1899*, new ed. (Eugene, Ore., 2007), 69.

7. George M. Marsden, *Fundamentalism and American Culture*, new ed. (New York, 2006), 35–38.

8. H. W. Smith, *The Christian's Secret of a Happy Life*, rev. ed. (Boston, 1885), 243.

9. D. L. Moody, *Secret Power; or, The Secret of Success in Christian Life and Christian Work* (Chicago, 1881), 111.

10. Milton C. Sernett, ed., *African American Religious History: A Documentary Witness*, 2nd ed. (Durham, N.C., 1999), 270, 273; Anne H. Pinn and Anthony B. Pinn, *Fortress Introduction to Black Church History* (Minneapolis, 2002), 112–13.

11. Grant Wacker, "The Holy Spirit and the Spirit of the Age in American Protestantism, 1880–1910," *Journal of American History* 72, no. 1 (June 1985): 45–46.

12. Marsden, *Fundamentalism and American Culture*, 34.

13. Candy Gunther Brown, *The Word in the World: Evangelical Writing, Publishing, and Reading in America, 1789–1880* (Chapel Hill, N.C., 2004), 211–12.

14. Catherine B. Allen, *The New Lottie Moon Story* (Nashville, 1980), 160.

15. Robert E. Speer, "The Evangelization of the World in This Generation," in *The Student Missionary Appeal* (New York, 1898), 206.

16. Walter A. McDougall, *The Tragedy of U.S. Foreign Policy: How America's Civil Religion Betrayed the National Interest* (New Haven, Conn., 2016), 123–24.

17. William R. Hutchinson, *Errand to the World: American Protestant Thought and Foreign Missions* (Chicago, 1987), 135; Brian Stanley, *The World Missionary Conference, Edinburgh 1910* (Grand Rapids, Mich., 2009), 99; Thomas S. Kidd, *American Christians and Islam: Evangelical Culture and Muslims from the Colonial Period to the Age of Terrorism* (Princeton, N.J., 2009), 58–66.

18. Benjamin L. Hartley, *Evangelicals at a Crossroads: Revivalism and Social Reform in Boston, 1860–1910* (Hanover, N.H., 2011), 23–24.

19. Barry Hankins, *Jesus and Gin: Evangelicalism, the Roaring Twenties and Today's Culture Wars* (New York, 2010), 30; Brendan J. Payne, "Defending Black Suffrage: Poll Taxes, Preachers, and Anti-Prohibition in Texas, 1887–1916," *Journal of Southern History* 83, no. 4 (Nov. 2017): 850–51.

20. "Hillyer Resolutions, Chattanooga, Tennessee—1906," http://www.sbc.net/resolutions/688/hillyer-resolutions; Joe L. Coker, *Liquor in the Land of the Lost Cause: Southern White Evangelicals and the Prohibition Movement* (Lexington, Ky., 2007), 150–51.

21. Amy Louise Wood, *Lynching and Spectacle: Witnessing Racial Violence in America, 1890–1940* (Chapel Hill, N.C., 2009), 61; Rebecca Burns, *Rage in the Gate City: The Story of the 1906 Atlanta Race Riot*, rev. ed. (Athens, Ga., 2009), 168.

22. Leonard J. Moore, *Citizen Klansmen: The Ku Klux Klan in Indiana, 1921–1928* (Chapel Hill, N.C., 1991), 75; Darren E. Grem, "Sam Jones, Sam Hose, and the Theology of Racial Violence," *Georgia Historical Quarterly* 90, no. 1 (Spring 2006): 58.

23. James H. Cone, *The Cross and the Lynching Tree* (Maryknoll, N.Y., 2011), 132, 141; Mary Beth Swetnam Mathews, *African American Evangelicals and Fundamentalism between the Wars* (Tuscaloosa, Ala., 2017), 148.

24. Coker, *Liquor in the Land*, 154.

25. J. Gresham Machen, *Christianity and Liberalism*, new ed. (Grand Rapids, Mich., 2009), 2.

26. Allen, *New Lottie Moon Story*, 138–39.

27. Gregory Wills, *Southern Baptist Theological Seminary, 1859–2009* (New York, 2009), 122.

28. Marsden, *Fundamentalism and American Culture*, 71.

29. Molly Worthen, *Apostles of Reason: The Crisis of Authority in American Evangelicalism* (New York, 2014), 19–24.

30. Marsden, *Fundamentalism and American Culture*, 117; Bradley J. Gundlach, *Process and Providence: The Evolution Question at Princeton, 1845–1929* (Grand Rapids, Mich., 2013), 306–9.

31. Marsden, *Fundamentalism and American Culture*, 122–23.

32. Ferenc M. Szasz, "William Jennings Bryan, Evolution, and the Fundamentalist-Modernist Controversy," *Nebraska History* 56 (1975): 264–65; Susan L. Trollinger and William Vance Trollinger Jr., "The Bible and Creationism," in *The Oxford Handbook of the Bible in America*, ed. Paul C. Gutjahr (New York, 2017), 219; Barry Hankins, *American Evangelicals: A Contemporary History of a Mainstream Religious Movement* (Lanham, Md., 2008), 73–75.

33. Michael Kazin, *A Godly Hero: The Life of William Jennings Bryan* (New York, 2006), 277.

34. Charles A. Israel, *Before Scopes: Evangelicalism, Education, and Evolution in Tennessee, 1870–1925* (Athens, Ga., 2004), 141–42.

35. Edward J. Larson, *Summer for the Gods: The Scopes Trial and America's Continuing Debate over Science and Religion*, rev. ed. (New York, 2006), 148–49.

36. S. T. Joshi, ed., *H. L. Mencken on Religion* (Amherst, N.Y., 2010), 136, 219.

37. Szasz, "Bryan," 275.

4
The Neo-Evangelical Movement and Billy Graham

1. Barry Hankins, *American Evangelicals: A Contemporary History of a Mainstream Religious Movement* (Lanham, Md., 2008), 33–35; Jeffrey S. McDonald, *John Gerstner and the Renewal of Presbyterian and Reformed Evangelicalism in Modern America* (Eugene, Ore., 2017), 7. In the mid-twentieth century the PCUSA was known as the United Presbyterian Church in the USA.

2. Garth M. Rosell, *The Surprising Work of God: Harold John Ockenga, Billy Graham, and the Rebirth of Evangelicalism* (Grand Rapids, Mich., 2008), 93–98.

3. Daniel K. Williams, *God's Own Party: The Making of the Christian Right* (New York, 2010), 12, 16–17.

4. Miles Mullin, "The Quandary of African American Evangelicalism," *Anxious Bench* blog, Feb. 6, 2013, http://www.patheos.com/blogs/anxious bench/2013/02/the-quandary-of-african-american-evangelicalism/; Soong-Chan Rah, "In Whose Image: The Emergence, Development, and Challenge

of African-American Evangelicalism" (Ph.D. diss., Duke University, 2016), 182–90.

5. Gastón Espinosa, *Latino Pentecostals in America: Faith and Politics in Action* (Cambridge, Mass., 2014), 101–2.

6. Espinosa, *Latino Pentecostals*, 109–10, 130–32.

7. Aimee Semple McPherson, *This Is That: Personal Experiences, Sermons, and Writings* (Los Angeles, 1919), 636; Matthew Avery Sutton, *Aimee Semple McPherson and the Resurrection of Christian America* (Cambridge, Mass., 2007), 50–52.

8. Brian K. Pipkin, "The Foursquare Church and Pacifism," in *Pentecostals and Nonviolence: Reclaiming a Heritage*, ed. Paul Nathan Alexander (Eugene, Ore., 2012), 106; Grant Wacker, *Heaven Below: Early Pentecostals and American Culture* (Cambridge, Mass., 2001), 218.

9. Anthea D. Butler, "Unrespectable Saints: Women of the Church of God in Christ," in *The Religious History of American Women: Reimagining the Past*, ed. Catherine A. Brekus (Chapel Hill, N.C., 2007), 175.

10. St. Clair Drake and Horace A. Clayton, *Black Metropolis: A Study of Negro Life in a Northern City*, rev. ed. (Chicago, 1993), 414; Alan Young, *Woke Me Up This Morning: Black Gospel Singers and the Gospel Life* (Jackson, Miss., 1997), 11; Jerma A. Jackson, *Singing in My Soul: Black Gospel Music in a Secular Age* (Chapel Hill, N.C., 2004), 28–34.

11. Theodore Kornweibel Jr., "Race and Conscientious Objection in World War I: The Story of the Church of God in Christ," in *Proclaim Peace: Christian Pacifism from Unexpected Quarters*, ed. Theron F. Schlabach and Richard T. Hughes (Urbana, Ill., 1997), 58–75.

12. Pearl S. Buck, "Is There a Case for Foreign Missions?" *Harper's*, Jan. 1933, 149.

13. Douglas A. Sweeney, *The American Evangelical Story: A History of the Movement* (Grand Rapids, Mich., 2005), 100; Thomas S. Kidd, *American Christians and Islam: Evangelical Culture and Muslims from the Colonial Period to the Age of Terrorism* (Princeton, N.J., 2009), 76; Bradley J. Longfield, *The Presbyterian Controversy: Fundamentalists, Modernists, and Moderates* (New York, 1991), 203–4; David A Hollinger, *Protestants Abroad: How Missionaries Tried to Change the World but Changed America* (Princeton, N.J., 2017), 69–70.

14. Paul Emory Putz, "God, Country, and Big-Time Sports: American Protestants and the Creation of 'Sportianity,' 1920–1980" (Ph.D. diss., Baylor University, 2018), 37.

15. D. G. Hart, *Recovering Mother Kirk: The Case for Liturgy in the Reformed Tradition* (Eugene, Ore., 2003), 146; Joel A. Carpenter, *Revive Us Again: The*

Reawakening of American Fundamentalism (New York, 1997), 180–81; Axel R. Schäfer, *Countercultural Conservatives: American Evangelicalism from the Postwar Revival to the New Christian Right* (Madison, Wisc., 2011), 57–58.

16. "Foreign Mission Board Appoints New Missionaries; Brings Total to 748," *Baptist Press*, Mar. 20, 1950; Ruth A. Tucker, *From Jerusalem to Irian Jaya: A Biographical History of Christian Missions*, 2nd ed. (Grand Rapids, Mich., 2004), 354; Melani McAlister, *The Kingdom of God Has No Borders: A Global History of American Evangelicals* (New York, 2018), 22.

17. Carpenter, *Revive Us Again*, 184.

18. George M. Marsden, *Reforming Fundamentalism: Fuller Seminary and the New Evangelicalism* (Grand Rapids, Mich., 1987), 53–68.

19. Carl F. H. Henry, *The Uneasy Conscience of Modern Fundamentalism* (Grand Rapids, Mich., 1947), 17, 88.

20. Andrew Finstuen, "Professor Graham: Billy Graham's Missions to Colleges and Universities," in *Billy Graham: American Pilgrim*, ed. Andrew Finstuen, Anne Blue Wills, and Grant Wacker (New York, 2017), 24.

21. Carpenter, *Revive Us Again*, 217; Ian M. Randall, "Billy Graham, Evangelism, and Fundamentalism," in *Evangelicalism and Fundamentalism in the United Kingdom during the Twentieth Century*, ed. David W. Bebbington and David Ceri Jones (Oxford, 2013), 180.

22. Grant Wacker, *America's Pastor: Billy Graham and the Shaping of a Nation* (Cambridge, Mass., 2014), 74–75.

23. Kate Bowler, *Blessed: A History of the American Prosperity Gospel* (New York, 2013), 28; Lerone Martin, "Bureau Clergyman: How the FBI Colluded with an African American Televangelist to Destroy Martin Luther King, Jr.," *Religion and American Culture* 28, no. 1 (2018): 7–8, 14–15; Gastón Espinosa, "Fierro, Robert Felix (1916–85)," in *The New International Dictionary of Pentecostal and Charismatic Movements*, ed. Stanley M. Burgess and Eduard M. van der Mass (Grand Rapids, Mich., 2002), 637–38; Espinosa, *Latino Pentecostals*, 238–39.

24. Candy Gunther Brown, "Healing Words: Narratives of Spiritual Healing and Kathryn Kuhlman's Uses of Print Culture, 1947–76," in *Religion and the Culture of Print in Modern America*, ed. Charles L. Cohen and Paul S. Boyer (Madison, Wisc., 2008), 271–74; Arlene Sánchez Walsh, *Pentecostals in America* (New York, 2018), 88–91.

25. Billy Graham, *The Holy Spirit: Activating God's Power in Your Life* (New York, 1978), 81.

26. Steven P. Miller, *Billy Graham and the Rise of the Republican South* (Philadelphia, 2009), 22.

27. Kevin M. Kruse, *One Nation under God: How Corporate America Invented Christian America* (New York, 2015), 58.

28. Kruse, *One Nation under God*, 57–61, 64, 72–75; Williams, *God's Own Party*, 27.

5
Two-Track Evangelicals and the New Christian Right

1. Susan Friend Harding, *The Book of Jerry Falwell: Fundamentalist Language and Politics* (Princeton, N.J., 2000), 285n18.

2. Angela M. Lahr, *Millennial Dreams and Apocalyptic Nightmares: The Cold War Origins of Political Evangelicalism* (New York, 2007), 117.

3. George Dugan, "100,000 Fill Yankee Stadium to Hear Graham," *New York Times*, July 21, 1957; Daniel K. Williams, *God's Own Party: The Making of the Christian Right* (New York, 2010), 49.

4. Kevin M. Kruse, *One Nation under God: How Corporate America Invented Christian America* (New York, 2015), 95–125.

5. Jonathan P. Herzog, *The Spiritual-Industrial Complex: America's Religious Battle against Communism in the Early Cold War* (New York, 2011), 187; Thomas S. Kidd and Barry Hankins, *Baptists in America: A History* (New York, 2015), 206–7; Matthew Bowman, *Christian: The Politics of a Word in America* (Cambridge, Mass., 2018), 186–87; Kruse, *One Nation under God*, 188–89.

6. Herzog, *Spiritual-Industrial Complex*, 188; Williams, *God's Own Party*, 64.

7. Williams, *God's Own Party*, 64; Kruse, *One Nation under God*, 200–201.

8. Williams, *God's Own Party*, 65; Martin Tolchin, "Amendment Drive on School Prayer Loses Senate Vote," *New York Times*, Mar. 21, 1984, A1.

9. Republican Party Platform, 2016, https://prod-cdn-static.gop.com/media/documents/DRAFT_12_FINAL[1]-ben_1468872234.pdf.

10. Charles Marsh, *God's Long Summer: Stories of Faith and Civil Rights* (Princeton, N.J., 1997), 45.

11. John Perkins, *Let Justice Roll Down* (Ventura, Calif., 1976), 72.

12. Albert G. Miller, "The Black Apostle to White Evangelicals," in *Mobilizing for the Common Good: The Lived Theology of John M. Perkins*, ed. Peter Slade, Charles Marsh, and Peter Goodwin Heltzel (Oxford, Miss., 2013), 4; Soong-Chan Rah, "In Whose Image: The Emergence, Development, and Challenge of African-American Evangelicalism" (Ph.D. diss., Duke University, 2016), 231–52.

13. Rah, "In Whose Image," 198.

14. Steven P. Miller, *Billy Graham and the Rise of the Republican South* (Philadelphia, 2009), 60, 128; Grant Wacker, *America's Pastor: Billy Graham and the Shaping of a Nation* (Cambridge, Mass., 2014), 126–29.

15. Peter Heltzel, *Jesus and Justice: Evangelicals, Race, and American Politics* (New Haven, Conn., 2009), 83.

16. David R. Swartz, *Moral Minority: The Evangelical Left in an Age of Conservatism* (Philadelphia, 2012), 31, 156.

17. Carolyn Renée Dupont, *Mississippi Praying: Southern White Evangelicals and the Civil Rights Movement, 1945–1975* (New York, 2013), 110; Williams, *God's Own Party*, 33–34; David L. Chappell, *A Stone of Hope: Prophetic Religion and the Death of Jim Crow* (Chapel Hill, N.C., 2004), 114–15; Timothy B. Tyson, *Blood Done Sign My Name: A True Story* (New York, 2004), 55–56.

18. William Martin, "God's Ambassador to the World," in *Billy Graham: American Pilgrim*, ed. Andrew Finstuen, Anne Blue Wills, and Grant Wacker (New York, 2017), 92.

19. Juan Francisco Martínez, *The Story of Latino Protestants in the United States* (Grand Rapids, Mich., 2018), 131–32.

20. Rah, "In Whose Image," 205–30.

21. Nancy Haught, "Evangelist Palau Drew Inspiration, Help from Graham," *Oregonian*, June 24, 2005, A13; David Stoll, *Is Latin America Turning Protestant? The Politics of Evangelical Growth* (Berkeley, Calif., 1990), 121–24.

22. Thomas S. Kidd, *American Christians and Islam: Evangelical Culture and Muslims from the Colonial Period to the Age of Terrorism* (Princeton, N.J., 2009), 127.

23. "The Lausanne Covenant," Aug. 1, 1974, https://www.lausanne.org/content/covenant/lausanne-covenant; Brian Stanley, " 'Lausanne 1974': The Challenge from the Majority World to Northern-Hemisphere Evangelicalism," *Journal of Ecclesiastical History* 64, no. 3 (July 2013), https://www.cambridge.org/core/journals/journal-of-ecclesiastical-history/article/lausanne-1974-the-challenge-from-the-majority-world-to-northernhemisphere-evangelicalism/9158C31B75F72327815F9EE28AF9DC22/core-reader.

24. Daniel Salinas, *Latin American Evangelical Theology in the 1970s: The Golden Decade* (Leiden, 2009), 142.

25. Philip Jenkins, *The Next Christendom: The Coming of Global Christianity*, rev. ed. (New York, 2007), 1–2; U.S. Census Bureau, "The Hispanic Population: 2010," May 2011, https://www.census.gov/prod/cen2010/briefs/c2010br-04.pdf.

26. U.S. Census Bureau, "The Asian Population: 2010," Mar. 2012, https://www.census.gov/prod/cen2010/briefs/c2010br-11.pdf; Rebecca Y. Kim, *The Spirit Moves West: Korean Missionaries in America* (New York, 2015), 31–36.

27. R. Stephen Warner, "Coming to America: Immigrants and the Faith They Bring," *Christian Century*, Feb. 10, 2004, 20–23; Jenkins, *Next Christendom*, 123–24.

28. Juan Martínez, "By the Numbers," August 15, 2012, Center for Religion and Civic Culture, University of Southern California, https://crcc.usc.edu/report/the-latino-church-next/by-the-numbers/.

29. "Sonny Arguinzoni," http://www.sonnyarguinzoni.org/; Luis León, "Born Again in East LA: The Congregation as Border Space," in *Gatherings in Diaspora: Religious Communities and the New Immigration*, ed. R. Stephen Warner and Judith G. Wittner (Philadelphia, 1998), 166–68.

30. Marilynn Johnson, "'The Quiet Revival': New Immigrants and the Transformation of Christianity in Greater Boston," *Religion and American Culture: A Journal of Interpretation* 24, no. 2 (July 2014): 241–45.

31. Johnson, "Quiet Revival," 245–46; Soong-Chan Rah, *The Next Evangelicalism: Releasing the Church from Western Cultural Captivity* (Downers Grove, Ill., 2009), 16–17.

32. J. Gordon Melton and Todd Ferguson, "America's Invisible Religion: The McLennan County Church Survey" (paper presented at the annual conference of the Association for the Study of Religion, Economics, and Culture held at Chapman University, Orange, Calif., Mar. 18–19, 2016).

33. Larry Eskridge, *God's Forever Family: The Jesus People Movement in America* (New York, 2013), 68–71.

34. Eskridge, *God's Forever Family*, 75, 265, 274.

35. Williams, *God's Own Party*, 94, 98–99; Wacker, *America's Pastor*, 222; Melani McAlister, *The Kingdom of God Has No Borders: A Global History of American Evangelicals* (New York, 2018), 64.

36. Williams, *God's Own Party*, 99, 102.

37. Williams, *God's Own Party*, 114–19; Daniel K. Williams, *Defenders of the Unborn: The Pro-Life Movement Before* Roe v. Wade (New York, 2016), 170; Fannie Lou Hamer, *The Speeches of Fannie Lou Hamer: To Tell It Like It Is*, ed. Maegan Parker Brooks and Davis W. Houck (Jackson, Miss., 2011), 133.

38. Williams, *God's Own Party*, 124–27; Steven P. Miller, *The Age of Evangelicalism: America's Born-Again Years* (New York, 2014), 45.

39. Williams, *God's Own Party*, 124; Darren Dochuk, *From Bible Belt to Sunbelt: Plain Folk Religion, Grassroots Politics, and the Rise of Evangelical Conservatism* (New York, 2011), 263.

40. D. Michael Lindsay, *Faith in the Halls of Power: How Evangelicals Joined the American Elite* (New York, 2007), xi.

41. Williams, *God's Own Party*, 155–58; Christian Smith, *American Evangelicalism: Embattled and Thriving* (Chicago, 1998), 200–201; Barry Hankins,

Francis Schaeffer and the Shaping of Evangelical America (Grand Rapids, Mich., 2008), 181.

42. Barry Hankins, *American Evangelicals: A Contemporary History of a Mainstream Religious Movement* (Lanham, Md., 2008), 143–44; Seth Dowland, *Family Values and the Rise of the Christian Right* (Philadelphia, 2015), 27.

43. Williams, *God's Own Party*, 174–75.

6

Evangelicalism from Reagan to Obama

1. Lyman Kellstedt et al., "Faith Transformed: Religion and American Politics from FDR to George W. Bush," in *Religion and American Politics: From the Colonial Period to the Present*, ed. Luke E. Harlow and Mark A. Noll, 2nd ed. (New York, 2007), 273; Neil J. Young, *We Gather Together: The Religious Right and the Problem of Interfaith Politics* (New York, 2015), 210–11; Daniel K. Williams, *God's Own Party: The Making of the Christian Right* (New York, 2010), 193.

2. Williams, *God's Own Party*, 177–78; W. Gardner Selby, "Ted Cruz Says Today, Roughly Half of Born-Again Christians Aren't Voting," *Politifact Texas*, Mar. 30, 2015, http://www.politifact.com/texas/statements/2015/mar/30/ted-cruz/ted-cruz-says-today-roughly-half-born-again-christ/; John Piper, "Christian, You Are Free Not to Vote," *Desiring God*, Nov. 3, 2016, https://www.desiringgod.org/messages/sons-of-freedom-and-joy/excerpts/christian-you-are-free-not-to-vote.

3. Barry Hankins, *Uneasy in Babylon: Southern Baptist Conservatives and American Culture* (Tuscaloosa, Ala., 2002), 17.

4. Thomas S. Kidd and Barry Hankins, *Baptists in America: A History* (New York, 2015), 232.

5. Peter Steinfels, "Baptists Dismiss Seminary Head in Surprise Move," *New York Times*, Mar. 11, 1994, A16.

6. Kidd and Hankins, *Baptists in America*, 237–39.

7. Russell D. Moore, *The Kingdom of Christ: The New Evangelical Perspective* (Wheaton, Ill., 2004), 25–31.

8. Kate Shellnutt, "Hundreds of New Churches Not Enough to Satisfy Southern Baptists," *Christianity Today*, June 9, 2017, https://www.christianitytoday.com/news/2017/june/southern-baptist-convention-churches-baptisms-sbc-acp.html.

9. *Association of Religion Data Archives*, "Presbyterian Church in America," n.d., http://www.thearda.com/Denoms/D_1305.asp; Administrative Committee PCA, "PCA Statistics Five Year Summary," n.d., http://www.pcaac.

org/resources/pca-statistics-five-year-summary/; Michael Luo, "Preaching the Word and Quoting the Voice," *New York Times*, Feb. 26, 2006, 29, 32; Jeffrey S. McDonald, *John Gerstner and the Renewal of Presbyterian and Reformed Evangelicalism in Modern America* (Eugene, Ore., 2017), 180.

10. *Association of Religion Data Archives*, "Church of God in Christ," n.d., http://www.thearda.com/Denoms/D_988.asp; Church of God in Christ, "About Us," http://www.cogic.org/about-company/; *Association of Religion Data Archives*, "Assemblies of God, General Council of the," n.d., http://www.thearda. com/Denoms/D_1021.asp; Flower Pentecostal Heritage Center, "Assemblies of God 2015 Statistics Released, Growth Spurred by Ethnic Transformation," June 24, 2016, https://ifphc.wordpress.com/2016/06/24/assemblies-of-god-2015-statistics-released-growth-spurred-by-ethnic-transformation/.

11. Gastón Espinosa, *Latino Pentecostals in America: Faith and Politics in Action* (Cambridge, Mass., 2014), 342–43, 364.

12. Gastón Espinosa, "Obama Threaded the Moral Needle of Latino Evangelicals in '08," National Hispanic Christian Leadership Conference, June 28, 2009, https://nhclc.org/obama-threaded-the-moral-needle-of-latino-evangelicals-in-08/; "After Praying at His Inauguration, Pastor Splits with Trump over Immigration Views," *National Public Radio*, Jan. 21, 2018, https://www.npr.org/2018/01/21/579584241/after-praying-at-his-inauguration-pastor-splits-with-trump-over-immigration-view.

13. "Conservative Spotlight: Dr. Tony Evans," *Human Events*, July 31, 2006, http://humanevents.com/2006/07/31/conservative-spotlight-dr-tony-evans/; Oak Cliff Bible Fellowship, "Dr. Tony Evans," https://www.ocbfchurch.org/boardofelders/tony-evans/.

14. Sarah Pulliam Bailey, "Why Women Want Moore," *Christianity Today* 54, no. 8 (Aug. 2010): 20–25; Kelsey Burke, "Why Beth Moore Walked It Back: This Election Season, It's Tough Being an Evangelical Woman," *Religion Dispatches*, Oct. 19, 2016, http://religiondispatches.org/why-beth-moore-walked-it-back-this-election-season-its-tough-being-an-evangelical-woman/.

15. "Comparison of 1925, 1963 and 2000 Baptist Faith and Message," *Southern Baptist Convention*, http://www.sbc.net/bfm2000/bfmcomparison.asp. Hybels retired early from Willow Creek in 2018 after allegations of inappropriate behavior toward a series of women. Manya Brachear Pashman and Jeff Coen, "Hybels Steps Down from Willow Creek Following Allegations of Misconduct," *Chicago Tribune*, Apr. 11, 2018, http://www.chicagotribune.com/news/local/breaking/ct-met-hybels-willow-creek-resigns-20180410-story.html.

16. For example, see Hannah Hartig, "Republicans Turn More Negative toward Refugees as Number Admitted to U.S. Plummets," Pew Research

Center, May 24, 2018, http://www.pewresearch.org/fact-tank/2018/05/24/
republicans-turn-more-negative-toward-refugees-as-number-admitted-to-
u-s-plummets/. Anthea Butler comments on the lack of media attention to
black evangelicals in Danielle Kurtzleben, "Are You an Evangelical? Are You
Sure?" *National Public Radio*, Dec. 19, 2015, https://www.npr.org/2015/12/19/
458058251/are-you-an-evangelical-are-you-sure.

17. Kurtzleben, "Are You an Evangelical?"

18. Steven P. Miller, *The Age of Evangelicalism: America's Born-Again Years*
(New York, 2014), 64; Williams, *God's Own Party*, 189.

19. Williams, *God's Own Party*, 217–20.

20. Brantley W. Gasaway, *Progressive Evangelicals and the Pursuit of Social
Justice* (Chapel Hill, N.C., 2014), 153–54.

21. Melani McAlister, *The Kingdom of God Has No Borders: A Global History of American Evangelicals* (New York, 2018), 137.

22. Williams, *God's Own Party*, 234; Miller, *Age of Evangelicalism*, 106–11;
Amy E. Black, "Evangelicals, Politics, and Public Policy: Lessons from the
Past, Prospects for the Future," in *The Future of Evangelicalism in America*,
ed. Candy Gunther Brown and Mark Silk (New York, 2016), 138–39.

23. M. Alex Johnson, "Bush—Born Again, or Not?" *NBC News*, Sept. 28,
2004, http://www.nbcnews.com/id/6115719/ns/politics/t/bush-born-again-
or-not/#.Ww188novyUk; Berkeley Center for Religion, Peace & World Affairs,
"George W. Bush on Christ Changing His Heart at the 1999 Iowa Republican
Presidential Debate," Dec. 13, 1999, https://berkleycenter.georgetown.edu/
quotes/george-w-bush-on-christ-changing-his-heart-at-the-1999-iowa
-republican-presidential-debate.

24. Williams, *God's Own Party*, 250–54.

25. Thomas S. Kidd, *American Christians and Islam: Evangelical Culture
and Muslims from the Colonial Period to the Age of Terrorism* (Princeton, N.J.,
2009), 145.

26. Williams, *God's Own Party*, 258–61, 266.

27. Stephen Labaton, "McCain Casts Muslims as Less Fit to Lead," *New
York Times*, Sept. 30, 2007, 22; John L. Esposito, *The Future of Islam* (New
York, 2010), 21–22.

28. Barack Obama, *The Audacity of Hope: Thoughts on Reclaiming the
American Dream* (New York, 2006), 208.

29. Richard A. Oppel Jr. and Erik Eckholm, "Prominent Pastor Calls
Romney's Church a Cult: Comments Cause Stir at a Forum for Conservatives,"
New York Times, Oct. 8, 2011, A10.

30. "Baptist Pastor Defends 'Cult' Description of Mormonism, Still Backs
Romney over Obama," *Fox News*, Oct. 9, 2011, http://www.foxnews.com/

politics/2011/10/09/baptist-pastor-defends-cult-description-mormonism-still-backs-romney-over-obama.html; John Fea, "The Court Evangelicals," *The Way of Improvement Leads Home*, May 6, 2017, https://thewayofimprovement. com/2017/05/06/the-court-evangelicals/.

Coda

1. Jessica Taylor, "Citing 'Two Corinthians,' Trump Struggles to Make the Sale to Evangelicals," *National Public Radio*, Jan. 18, 2016, https://www. npr.org/2016/01/18/463528847/citing-two-corinthians-trump-struggles-to-make-the-sale-to-evangelicals. Christians in Britain do conventionally say "Two Corinthians."

2. Emma Green, "Black Pastors Are Breaking the Law to Get Hillary Clinton Elected," *Atlantic*, Aug. 8, 2016, https://www.theatlantic.com/politics/archive/2016/08/black-pastors-pulpit-hillary-clinton/494876/.

3. Ryan P. Burge, "The 2016 Religious Vote (for More Groups Than You Thought Possible)," *Religion in Public*, Mar. 10, 2017, https://religioninpublic. blog/2017/03/10/the-2016-religious-vote-for-more-groups-than-you-thought-possible/; Leinz Vales, "Pastor First to Quit Trump's Evangelical Advisory Board: 'There Was a Line,' " *CNN*, Aug. 20, 2017, https://www.cnn. com/2017/08/19/politics/pastor-bernard-trump-evangelical-advisory-board-don-lemon-cnntv/index.html.

4. Seymour Institute, "An Open Letter to Hillary Clinton regarding Religious Freedom for Black America," https://www.seymourinstitute.com/open-letter.html.

5. Thabiti Anyabwile, "4 Problems Associated with White Evangelical Support of Donald Trump," *The Gospel Coalition*, Nov. 9, 2016, https://www. thegospelcoalition.org/blogs/thabiti-anyabwile/4-problems-associated-with-white-evangelical-support-of-donald-trump/.

6. For example, Paul A. Djupe, Jacob R. Neiheisel, and Anand Edward Sokhey, "How Fights over Trump Have Led Evangelicals to Leave Their Churches," *Washington Post*, Apr. 11, 2017; Janelle Wong, "This Is Why White Evangelicals Still Support Donald Trump. (It's Not Economic Anxiety)," *Washington Post*, June 19, 2018, https://www.washingtonpost.com/news/monkey-cage/wp/2018/06/19/white-evangelicals-still-support-donald-trump-because-theyre-more-conservative-than-other-evangelicals-this-is-why/?utm_term=.d7da5b2e0c97. On the definition of evangelicalism, see, for example, the roundtable on the "Bebbington quadrilateral" in *Fides et Historia* 47, no. 1 (Winter–Spring 2015): 44–96; Linford D. Fisher, "Evangelicals and Unevangelicals: The Contested History of a Word,

1500–1950," *Religion and American Culture* 26, no. 2 (Summer 2016): 184–226.

7. Ed Stetzer and Andrew MacDonald, "Why Evangelicals Voted Trump: Debunking the 81%," *Christianity Today*, Oct. 18, 2018, https://www.christianity today.com/ct/2018/october/why-evangelicals-trump-vote-81-percent-2016-election.html.

8. Bob Smietana, "LifeWay Research: Many Who Call Themselves Evangelical Don't Actually Hold Evangelical Beliefs," Dec. 6, 2017, https://blog.lifeway. com/newsroom/2017/12/06/lifeway-research-many-who-call-themselves-evangelical-dont-actually-hold-evangelical-beliefs/; Geoffrey Layman, "Where Is Trump's Evangelical Base? Not in Church," *Washington Post*, Mar. 29, 2016, https:// www.washingtonpost.com/news/monkey-cage/wp/2016/03/29/where-is-trumps-evangelical-base-not-in-church/?noredirect=on&utm_term=.212d1ae50ca4; Pew Research Center, "The Religious Typology: A New Way to Categorize Americans by Religion," Aug. 29, 2018, http://www.pewforum.org/2018/08/29/the-religious-typology/. This Pew study also struggled with low response rates: a December 2017 wave generated a 2.4 percent cumulative response rate. Conrad Hackett and D. Michael Lindsay, "Measuring Evangelicalism: Consequences of Different Operationalization Strategies," *Journal for the Scientific Study of Religion* 47, no. 3 (Sept. 2008): 512.

9. Robert Wuthnow, *Inventing American Religion: Polls, Surveys, and the Tenuous Quest for a Nation's Faith* (New York, 2015), 106–7.

10. Wuthnow, *Inventing American Religion*, 166–67; Scott Keeter, Nick Hatley, Courtney Kennedy, and Arnold Lau, "What Low Response Rates Mean for Telephone Surveys," Pew Research Center, May 15, 2017, http:// www.pewresearch.org/2017/05/15/what-low-response-rates-mean-for-telephone-surveys/.

11. Arthur C. Brooks, *Who Really Cares: The Surprising Truth about Compassionate Conservatism* (New York, 2006), 33–38.

12. Adelle M. Banks, "Homeless Find Rest in Faith-Based Shelters More Than Others," Religion News Service, Feb. 1, 2017, https://www.deseretnews. com/article/865672372/Homeless-find-rest-in-faith-based-shelters-more-than-others.html; "About the Association of Gospel Rescue Missions," http:// www.agrm.org/agrm/About_AGRM.asp.

13. Sarah Eekhoff Zylstra, "How Southern Baptists Trained More Disaster Relief Volunteers Than the Red Cross," *The Gospel Coalition*, Nov. 17, 2017, https://www.thegospelcoalition.org/article/how-southern-baptists-trained-more-disaster-relief-volunteers-than-the-red-cross/; Marshall Loeb, "How to Find the Right Child-Sponsorship Charity," *CBS News*, May 12, 2008, https:// www.cbsnews.com/news/how-to-find-the-right-child-sponsorship-charity/;

"About Compassion International," https://www.compassion.com/press/about-compassion.htm.

14. Brooks, *Who Really Cares*, 35; Perry Bacon Jr. and Amelia Thomson-DeVeaux, "How Trump and Race Are Splitting Evangelicals," *FiveThirtyEight*, Mar. 2, 2018, https://fivethirtyeight.com/features/how-trump-and-race-are-splitting-evangelicals/.

Index